AMERICA'S JAPAN

World War II: The Global, Human, and Ethical Dimension
G. KURT PIEHLER, SERIES EDITOR

AMERICA'S JAPAN

THE FIRST YEAR, 1945–1946

GRANT K. GOODMAN

Translated by Barry D. Steben

FORDHAM UNIVERSITY PRESS • NEW YORK • 2005

Copyright © 2005 Fordham University Press

America's Japan: The First Year, 1945–1946 was originally published in Japanese under the title *Amerika no Nippon Gannen 1945–1946,* © 1986, Otsuki Shoten Publishers.

World War II: The Global, Human, and Ethical Dimension, No. 7
ISSN 1541-0293

Library of Congress Cataloging-in-Publication Data

Goodman, Grant Kohn, 1924–
   America's Japan : the first year, 1945–1946 / Grant K. Goodman; translated by Barry D. Steben.— 1st ed.
      p. cm. — (World War II—the global, human, and ethical dimension, ISSN 1541-0293 ; 7)
   Translated from japanese "America no Nihon gannen" (translation of America's Japan [memoir])
   Includes bibliographical references and index.
ISBN 0-8232-2515-1 (hardcover)
   1. Japan—History—Allied occupation, 1945–1952. 2. Goodman, Grany Kohn, 1924–
I. Steben, Barry D. II. title. III. Series.
   DS889.16.G66 2005
   940.53'52'09045—dc22

2005016716

Designed by Brady McNamara
Text set 10.25/15 Janson
Printed in the United States of America
07 06 05 5 4 3 2 1
First edition

CONTENTS

✪

FOREWORD

✪

HUNDREDS OF MEMOIRS have been written by the men and women who participated in the (largely American) Allied Occupation of Japan (1945–1952). Among them, this book entices like a rare gem. Second Lieutenant Grant K. Goodman, then 21, was honest, brilliant, energetic, and, above all, enamored of a great cause: the democratization of Japan. He was not a passive observer. As an Army language officer, he translated hundreds of thousands of letters written by ordinary Japanese living under foreign occupation, and in so doing, he came to know their hearts and minds intimately.

The letters Goodman rendered into English must have further enhanced the proverbial self-esteem of General Douglas MacArthur, the Allied Supreme Commander, and contributed in their way to the success of his occupation project. As the author notes, "the Japanese were waiting for me." Together, they worked hard to build a democratic postwar nation. The time was right, and the fate of Japan had been entrusted to MacArthur's firm if somewhat grandiose helmsmanship.

Unlike the Iraqis of today, who have bitterly contested America's invasion and ongoing occupation of their country, the Japanese were eager to assist the Yankee occupier in remolding their lives and institutions. The conquerors, the author among them, were contented soldiers, proud to do their duty and assured of the esteem and cooperation of the occupied. American GIs in Japan never stooped to the villainy of torture, unlike their counterparts at Abu Ghraib.

Grant Goodman's compelling account of his experiences in occupied Japan is a must-read for those struggling to understand America's current failure in Iraq.

Rinjiro Sodei
PROFESSOR EMERITUS
HOSEI UNIVERSITY, TOKYO

IT IS REMARKABLE that in 2004, almost 60 years after the events described in these memoirs, the contents are as vivid to me as in 1945–1946. The impact of these experiences is so profound that I can recall each of them as though they occurred yesterday. As I look back on my unique military service, I realize how many factors contributed to my ability to recall the contents of what follows.

At age 18, I was undoubtedly at the zenith of my "intellectual" capacity. I was also and had always been an intensely conscientious as well as an intensely competitive student. My language learning competence had already encompassed Latin, French, Spanish, and Esperanto. My interest in Asia had been strong since my childhood, and my decision to attend Princeton University was the result of my interest in its Woodrow Wilson School of Public and International Affairs.

When Pearl Harbor was attacked, my patriotism was profoundly stimulated, and I was determined to serve my country in an appropriate fashion. Thus, to learn the Japanese language as my contribution to military service proved both logical and rewarding.

After some six decades, it is extremely difficult to put into words the truly tremendous enthusiasm and energy with which I applied myself in the Army Intensive Japanese Language School. Moreover, I believe that it was the same intense commitment which I brought to that first year of the Occupation of Japan.

Naively, perhaps, I believed utterly in what the Occupation intended, especially in the concept of democratizing the Japanese. I perceived myself in some sense as a secular missionary seeking to bring to the Japanese all of the wonderful benefits of the American system. I never doubted for a moment the righteousness of our cause or the correctness of our reform program. Indeed, I took personal pride in believing that I was one small part of a great crusade which would both transform Japan and guarantee the future peace of the world.

Grant K. Goodman
Lawrence, Kansas
August, 2004

AMERICA'S JAPAN

A Yen for Japan

LET ME BEGIN by talking of my memories about Japan from my childhood.

I was born in Cleveland on the 18th of October, 1924. Cleveland has long been known as a city of steel, which flourished because of the convenience of water transport through the Great Lakes.

When I look back, my first encounter with Japan was around the time of the "Manchurian Incident," that is, around 1931, when I was seven years old and in second grade. I was already able to read newspapers and magazines at that time, and I remember that I read the reports on the incident in the library and wrote a report about it for school, which I presented to the class. Yes, I was quite a precocious little pupil! Actually, since I was already very good at reading in kindergarten, the kindergarten teacher often left me alone to read to the class while she would sneak out of the room and smoke a cigarette.

After I did my report on the Manchurian Incident, I continued to read the newspaper reports of the increasingly tense relationship between Japan and China. As a result, I have an especially clear memory of the outbreak of the war between Japan and China on July 7, 1937. It seems that in this period I was reading a great many articles related to Japan in the newspapers and magazines.

There was another thing that generated my interested in Japan, or rather Asia as a whole—reading books together with my parents at home. My parents would choose the books, and then my father, my mother and I would take turns reading aloud to each other, each in turn responsible for a whole chapter. Of the many books I read this way, I think that *Oil for the Lamps of China*, by Alice Tisdale Hobart (1934), and *Lost Horizon* by James Hilton (1933), greatly stimulated my interest in Asia.

Since these two books were both best sellers in America in the 1930s, and they were made into movies, I think that they were also quite well known in Japan. Hobart's *Oil for the Lamps of China* is a story about Americans doing business in China, while Hilton's *Lost Horizon* is a love story that unfolds with a fantasy-world image of Tibet in the background. Neither of these books has a direct connection with Japan, but since I can still recall their titles and content after some seventy years, it is obvious that they had a great impact on my youthful fascination with Asia.

Other factors that fed my early interest in Japan were my matchbox-label collection and my stamp collection. At the time, among my family's friends there was a somewhat mysterious adventurer who seemingly traveled around the world a great deal. He used to drop in at our home about once a year, and once he brought me a matchbox-label collection book from

Japan, giving birth to my interest in this sort of thing. Before the Second World War, Japan, of course, was a major exporter of sundry goods, and Japanese matches flooded the world market. The labels of the matchboxes had East Asian-style paintings, national flags, and other designs printed on them, and on the sides was written the name of the city of manufacture—Kobe, Osaka, and so on. At the time a lot of people made a hobby of collecting these labels, like collecting stamps or coins. When I looked at the matchbox labels that adventurer gave me, I could get romantic glimpses of a Japan which I could only imagine.

My stamp collection was also very useful in deepening my knowledge of Japan. At the time my father was a businessman who dealt in cloth products, and he handled textiles imported from Japan. Thus, I was able to obtain many Japanese stamps. My stamp collection included a stamp issued, I think, about 1935 with a picture of Japan's puppet emperor in Manchuria, Pu Yi, and other stamps associated with Manchukuo like those carrying the name of the new capital.

In this way, while enjoying myself, I gained a lot of knowledge about the history and geography of Japan, or Japan and Manchukuo, and when I became a senior high school student at the end of the 1930s, I had already made up my mind to do Japanese studies in university. At that time, the relations between Japan and the U.S. were beginning to get tense. In September 1939 the war between Germany and Poland broke out, and a year later the Japanese army occupied the northern part of French Indo-China. Four days later the tripartite alliance was concluded among Japan, Germany, and fascist Italy. With the expansion of the war in Europe, the shadow of the war between Japan and China began to spread over Southeast Asia, and the antagonism to America grew rapidly more acute.

2

My First Study of Japanese—My Matriculation at Princeton University

AT THE END OF 1941, during the final term of senior high
school, I applied to Princeton University. I had heard that
Princeton offered a special course called "Public and International Affairs," and I thought that by choosing this course I
would be able to pursue the interests that I had had since my
youth. This means that I took the Princeton entrance exams in
the spring of 1942 and entered the university in the autumn of
the same year. Thus, needless to say, I had heard about Pearl
Harbor in December of the previous year, that is, during the
last term before my graduation from high school.

It was Sunday, the seventh of December, 1941. I was listening to the radio in my room, when suddenly a news bulletin
came on the air.

"The Japanese military have attacked Pearl Harbor!" I ran
downstairs to the living room where my family was gathered

together and said to everyone, "They say the Japanese have just attacked Pearl Harbor! This means war!"

Everyone was shocked, and they immediately switched on the radio to catch the bulletins. I still remember what my father said. "Grant, you will have to join the army, won't you?"

In the end, just like my father said, when I reached eighteen, I joined the army. But at the time of the news bulletin I had just passed my seventeenth birthday, and I had no idea I might join the army someday.

I remember how I answered, "Eh? I have to join the army??"

I graduated from high school in January of 1942. Since at that time, unlike today, the only time you could enter university was September, I had to wait for half a year. During that time I followed a postgraduate study program at the high school. Since I already had all the required credits, I chose courses like French, typing, and so on.

While I was pursuing these studies, I also joined a civil air raid warden brigade organized for defense in the event of air raids on the U.S. mainland by German or Japanese warplanes. As a member of this brigade, I made my rounds of the homes in the neighborhood wearing a helmet with "air-raid lookout brigade member" written on the side, checking whether they had prepared their air-raid shelters properly, whether they had prepared buckets of sand and water, whether they had enough shovels, and so on.

In retrospect, this was all needless effort, of course, but at the time there were all kinds of rumors flying around saying that the Germans had long-distance bombers that could reach American mainland, that the Japanese had secret weapons that were beyond our power to imagine, and so on. We took these rumors very seriously, so we devoted ourselves fervently to our training.

In September, 1942, I entered Princeton University, and the university life I had been looking forward to finally begin. But the war was already casting a dark cloud over the campus. When one reached eighteen, whether one liked it or not, one had to join the army.

I was lucky that I was only seventeen at the time. I would reach my eighteenth birthday in the middle of the first semester, and after the beginning of the next semester in January of 1943, I could be called into the army at any time if I were drafted.

I think it was just at the outset of that second semester that I heard that the army had a program for training intelligence officers who could speak Japanese. As soon as I read this call for volunteers on the campus bulletin board, I immediately resolved to apply to the program. I had two reasons. One was, needless to say, I already had a strong interest in Japan and this was the ideal chance to learn Japanese. The other was that if one applied for this program, one's conscription would be postponed, and one would have the privilege of taking whatever courses one wanted in the army after conscription.

However, even if one applied, not everyone was accepted. Only those who made it through a difficult test would be permitted to enter the Japanese language study program. It was even necessary to study some Japanese to pass the interview examination. So I got together with four other students, and we asked the university to allow us to study Japanese. However, unfortunately, there was no one who taught Japanese in Princeton at the time. Of course there were teachers with influence like Professor Philip Hitti, the distinguished Arabist, but because he was responsible for the Division of Middle and Near East Studies and specialized in Arabic problems, while he was generous in offering his support, he was not able to teach us Japanese.

So I asked Professor Hitti to help, and he put in a request to Professor Shirato Ichiro of Columbia University, about an hour away, to come to Princeton to give lessons. So I commenced my daily "special instruction" in Japanese from January, 1943, under Professor Shirato.

From January to March was the two-and-a-half-month period of my literal "special instruction," and I dropped all of my other studies to concentrate solely on Japanese. The textbook we used was the *Naganuma Reader*, which was used before the war for Japanese training at the American embassy in Tokyo. "Does this streetcar go to Hibiya?" was the first Japanese sentence I learned from this text.

It was in March 1943 that I was informed that an interview examination would be held for recruiting candidates for the army's Japanese language school. I was interviewed by a Lieutenant Colonel Stewart at the Bellview Stratford Hotel in Philadelphia. Lieutenant Colonel Stewart had been a Japanese language officer attached to the U.S. Embassy in Tokyo before the Pacific War, and he was interned at the time of the outbreak of the war. At the time of the interview he had just returned from Japan aboard a Japan-U.S. exchange ship. When he returned, he was enlisted into the Army's Japanese language training program and appointed as the official in charge of the interview examination. He conducted interview examinations in the eastern cities, starting in New York and moving on to Philadelphia and Baltimore.

The interview exam was held in a small room in the Bellview Stratford Hotel. All of the five Princeton students who had worked with Professor Shirato were interviewed at the same time. The room was so small that two of us had to sit on opposite ends of the bed. After he asked me, in Japanese, about my background and my age, and so on, he asked me two or three extremely simple questions. After my two-and-a-half months of "special instruction," of course, I was able to answer them without a hitch. The interview was over in a short time. Interestingly, of the five Princeton interviewees, Colonel Stewart selected three of us, of whom I was one.

A week later I was informed that I had passed the examination for the Japanese language training program. Thereupon I quickly returned to my hometown, went through the formal procedures for joining the army, and headed for the University of Michigan for my Japanese language education.

3

My Memories of the Army
Intensive Japanese Language School—
The University of Michigan

IN MARCH OF 1943, I left Princeton, suspending my studies, and returned to my home in Cleveland. In April I completed the enlistment procedures and headed for the University of Michigan. I packed a few daily necessities like a razor, a comb, and a toothbrush into my bag, and my parents saw me off on the train at Cleveland Terminal. On that day, a swearing-in ceremony was held in the Cleveland Public Square for several hundred men who were also joining the army, and the railroad station was teeming with parents and siblings seeing off young men departing on the same train for their places of assignment. I can remember the scene like it happened yesterday.

The train headed for Camp Perry in Ohio. This was the relay point from which soldiers were sent out to various destinations. After staying there for about ten days, I bade farewell to the other new recruits and went to the Army Intensive Japanese Language School at the University of Michigan to be trained as an intelligence officer, whose job it would be to translate Japanese documents, interrogate Japanese prisoners, and intercept communications in Japanese.

Incidentally, when I mention Camp Perry, those who know anything about Japanese history may think it has some connection with Commodore Perry, the commander of the "Black Ships" who forced the opening of Japan back in 1853-54. However, Commodore Perry's name was Matthew Galbraith Perry, while the Commodore Perry commemorated in the name of the camp was Oliver Hazard Perry. Oliver Perry was the naval commander who vanquished the British troops in the Battle of Lake Erie in the War of 1812, suddenly giving him the status of a national hero.

From Camp Perry I proceeded to the University of Michigan, which is in Ann Arbor, not far from Detroit, the great automotive city on the shores of Lake Michigan. It was in May of 1943 that I commenced my Japanese language training there. As I mentioned earlier, we received a little over a year of "intensive training" in Japanese, from May 1943 to May 1944.

In 1943, at the height of the Second World War, a great many young American men were shedding their blood in Europe, Asia, the Atlantic Ocean, or the Pacific Ocean in order to vanquish fascism and militarism. At such a busy and demanding time in the nation's history, we had been taken away from the fray to take a year of intensive training in Japanese. Depending on how one looks at it, it may look like the country had a lot of time to spare, but from another point of view, it shows how America was expecting the war with Japan to last a long time.

The director of the curriculum at the Army Intensive Japanese Language School at the University of Michigan was Joseph Yamagiwa, a professor in the Department of English Literature at the same university. Professor Yamagiwa was a second-generation

Japanese born in Maine, where very few people of Japanese descent lived. So a second-generation Japanese from Maine was a rare individual indeed. Professor Yamagiwa obtained his Ph.D. in Shakespearean studies from the University of Michigan in about 1940. Thus, until the opening of the Army Intensive Japanese Language School in January 1943, he had been a professor in English literature in the field of Shakespearean studies. As his background reveals, he had no connection whatever with Japanese Studies. However, when he took his doctorate in 1940, on the recommendation of Professor Robert B. Hall, he went to Japan to study Japanese as a foreign student. Robert B. Hall was a professor of geography at the University of Michigan, and he had deep knowledge regarding the geography of Japan. And more than anything, he had a very keen insight when it came to foreseeing developments in international affairs. On the basis of his judgment that war between America and Japan was unavoidable in the near future, he sent Professor Yamagiwa to Japan to learn Japanese, and had him come back to the U.S. on the eve of the outbreak of war and set him up as the pivotal person in the University of Michigan's newly founded Japanese language program. This was the kind of "magic" that perhaps only Robert B. Hall was capable of pulling off. Professor Yamagiwa was a young man who had just completed his Ph.D., but at Hall's instigation, he managed to master Japanese in two years in Japan, get married to a Japanese woman he met there, and make it safely back to the U.S. with his wife—just on the verge of the outbreak of hostilities. Since at the outbreak of the Pacific War, the U.S. had an extremely small number of Japan experts, Hall and Yamagiwa, after his return, appealed to the government to set up a Japanese language program at the University of Michigan, and went on to carry the project to realization.

Looking back, one must say that the choice of the University of Michigan was extremely perspicacious. After all, the majority of the male students were being drafted and heading off for the front, so that we could make full use of the extensive facilities of the university campus for our "special training," from dormitories to classrooms and from libraries to cafeterias.

My own intensive Japanese training began in May of 1943. The Japanese teachers, with the exception of Professor Yamagiwa, were first- and second-generation Japanese-Americans specially selected from the internment camps for Japanese-Americans, or second-generation Japanese men and women who had been born in the U.S. but had gone to Japan for their high school education. Needless to say, there was virtually no one among them who already had experience as a teacher of anything, and most of them had been housewives, small shop owners, fishermen, farmers, and so on, before their internment. Nevertheless, all of these individuals proved to be committed and even skilled teachers of the Japanese language. From their point of view, this job of teaching Japanese in the Army Intensive Japanese Language School must have been a great deal better than living a life without freedom in the forced internment camps. In Ann Arbor they could live completely independently and without any kind of physical limitation.

My favorite teachers were named Miss Kasahara, Mr. Nishio, Mr. Sakamoto, and Mr. Tanabe. It is with much nostalgia that I recall the names of these instructors who taught us Japanese, but at the beginning they had absolutely no experience as teachers. Professor Yamagiwa played the pivotal role in designing and implementing a curriculum consisting of conversational Japanese, literary Japanese, colloquial Japanese, grammar, Japanese history, and Japanese psychology. Training these neophytes to be teachers was also essential.

Incidentally, I am sometimes told that my Japanese language is feminine and very polite. The reason it is said to be feminine, I would think, is that I was often taught at the army school by a female teacher. The reason it is said to be polite is that in the classroom we learned a stiff and bookish kind of Japanese and had few opportunities to learn a really smooth and natural form of the language. This is hardly something peculiar to my own case, but a characteristic seen frequently among Americans who learn Japanese in schools and universities.

If our teachers had highly variegated backgrounds, this was no less true of the students. Most of those who had been selected were over twenty years old. At eighteen, I was part of the youngest group. Edward Norbeck—who later became a famous anthropologist after the war and retired from Rice University— was forty at the time, and there were a few others in his age group, so the age range was really quite broad.

The professions of the students before they entered the school also varied widely. Some had been students, while others had been university professors, lawyers, businessmen, teachers, and even laborers. Quite a bunch! All of them in their own unique way had come in contact with the Japanese language and had become seriously interested in it. Some of them had studied Japanese entirely on their own, through their own interest, neither through working at nor studying at a university, while some had been born in Japan and learned Japanese there. Those who had been born in Japan—whom we called BIJs—were also a varied bunch, including the sons of missionaries, the sons of businessmen, the sons of government officials, and so on. The more unusual included a teacher of classical ballet who had gone to Japan to teach Western classical dance and learned Japanese during his four or five years there, and a young man who had gone to Japan to practice Zen Buddhism. There were also two

or three who were of mixed Japanese and American parentage—
and in every case it was the mother who was Japanese.

Truly, students and teachers of a great variety of backgrounds came together at the Army Intensive Japanese Language School. If all of them had one thing in common, it was
the fact that the atmosphere that had nourished them was stimulating and positive, and all of them were brimming with enthusiasm and intelligence.

What about the content of our classes? We had a total of
five hours of class a day, from 8:00 to 12:00 in the morning,
and another hour after lunch from 1:00 to 2:00. Those five
hours were crammed full with courses in conversation, literary
Japanese, colloquial speech, *kanji* (Japanese characters), grammar, and dictation. While language learning was the core of
the curriculum, as mentioned previously, it also incorporated
Japanese history and Japanese psychology. In particular, we
studied the work of the famous British anthropologist Geoffrey Gorer, and I can remember fascinating lectures on things
like Japanese toilet-training and the character formation of
young children. According to Gorer, Japanese mothers, in
comparison with those in other cultures, toilet-train their
young children early, and this cultivates an authoritarian character that supposedly gave rise to Japanese militarism. We students had discussions and debates about this "revolutionary"
theory of Japanese psychology. Every evening we had required
study for two hours after dinner from 7:00 to 9:00. Needless to
say, as we were in the army, in the afternoon after our lectures
we also had military training. The dictionaries that we used
were Kenkyusha's *New Japanese-English Dictionary*, as well as
Meiseisha's *Kan'ei jiten* (Dictionary of Chinese Characters
Explained in English), edited by Arthur Rose Innes. I still
love to use both of these dictionaries regularly. Of course, we

were prohibited from using any language other than Japanese in class.

Then every Saturday morning we would have examinations. Conversation exams, colloquial speech exams, grammar exams, etc. In the afternoon the results of the exams would be posted, and reassignment to classes for the following week would be carried out in accord with the grading order. Each class had from about ten to twenty students, and the classes were formed by dividing students into eight or nine sections according to their grades on the exams. Every week, based on the results of the exam, some students would be transferred to a lower section, some students would move up, and some would stay in the same class. So the composition of the classes changed to some extent every week.

Throughout the entire year of the course, I maintained my place in Section One. I think I was able to do this because I was young and had a good memory, because I had studied Latin for four years from junior to senior high school and had mastered certain techniques for learning languages, and because I had familiarized myself with the Japanese language very early. But I also think that it was due to my intense personal eagerness to learn the language. I was studying, after all, not just because of the war, but because I saw this as the first step in my long-term life plan of becoming a Japan specialist. Among those who graduated from this wartime course, there were many who became university professors, lawyers, businessmen, authors, foreign service officers, members of Congress, and Christian ministers. From this alone it is obvious how many highly talented men were brought together in the Army Intensive Japanese Language School and used it ultimately as the springboard for their careers.

While the competition in the special training course was fierce, we did have our share of fun. One thing was the large number of movies that were screened to support our Japanese study. Movies I can remember now include *In the Case of the Wife* (*Tsuma no baai*) and *China Nights* (*Shina no yoru*). Of course, before the war, a large number of Japanese movies were imported, and they were shown in movie houses in cities with large Japanese populations like Los Angeles, San Francisco, and Seattle. However, with the outbreak of hostilities and the freezing of Japanese assets in America, the public showing of Japanese movies was prohibited and the films were confiscated by the U.S. government. The movies that we saw were these confiscated films, and since they were films released between about 1935 and 1940, they were quite new at the time.

The theme song of the movie *China Nights*, along with the acting skill of the Japanese-Chinese super-star Ri Koran (Shirley Yamaguchi) really fulfilled our dream images of the Far East, and the screaming cry of the child actor in *In the Case of the Wife*, "Okaachan! Okaachan!" ("Mama! Mama!"), immediately became the vogue-word among us students. At times when we were in a tight situation of one sort or another, we would shout "Okaachan, Okaachan!" as a sort of joke.

In addition, we loved to sing *Kimi ga yo*, the Japanese national anthem, as well as all kinds of Japanese army and navy songs, not to mention Japanese popular songs. In this way, I think, we made the curriculum of the Army Intensive Japanese Language School a lot more interesting for all of us.

Moreover, since almost all of the male students at the University of Michigan had been drafted, the only students left at the University of Michigan were the girls and those men with physical disabilities, who could not enter the army. We were practically the only male students left in Ann Arbor. Accordingly, not only in the university, but in the town as well, we were given a great welcome, and, even though we were in the middle of

World War Two, we were able to enjoy a time of "peace" very different from the bloody images of tanks, battleships, cannons and massacres that we usually associate with wars.

In May 1944, I graduated from my year-plus course at the Army Intensive Japanese Language School with top grades, having obtained "A" grades in thirty semester-hour credits. Since the normal number of semester hours per year in U.S. undergraduate university courses at that time was thirty, this means that I got through a full year of university with straight "A" grades.

So, as I have said, my year at the Army Intensive Japanese Language School was a time in which I made many good friends and enjoyed a stimulating intellectual environment. After I completed my four-and-a-half years of military service in October 1946 and left Japan to return to Princeton University, university life seemed boring by comparison and the students immature.

4

Practical Training—
Fort McClellan and Fort Snelling

AFTER WE GRADUATED from the Army Intensive Japanese Language School in May 1944, we were sent to Fort McClellan in Alabama to receive two months' infantry training. I'm not sure how long it took to get there by train, but Fort McClellan is in eastern Alabama near the town of Anniston.

In sharp contrast to our life of language study at the University of Michigan, here we spent day and night doing physical drill like calisthenics and running, as well as battle training. Shooting practice, gas-mask operation training, and belly-crawling were essential to our infantry-type training.

Although ordinary soldiers devote all their time to battle training, we had not moved on to that stage until after a year of language classes. Accordingly, these two months of rigorous physical training tended to squeeze us—as "top-heavy" as we had tended to become—to the limit. But it was a good way to heal our brains, which were tired from all that language training.

In August of 1944 we finished our two months of training and were sent to Fort Snelling in Minnesota near Minneapolis. Fort Snelling was the site of an army base that boasted a long history, starting with its function as a fortress at the time of the wars with the Indians. Here we entered a Military Intelligence Service Language Training School and continued our Japanese language studies for another half-year.

This school was distinguished, I suppose, by its dedication to the task of specialized language training for the purpose of gathering military intelligence. The Army Intensive Japanese Language School was connected to a university, and it gave mostly basic language training centering on daily life, while the Fort Snelling Military Intelligence Service Language School, as its name quite clearly implied, focused on training for the actual war theater, that is, military vocabulary, words used for distinguishing airplanes, the interception and deciphering of military telegraph messages, and the interception and deciphering of broadcasts in Japanese. This specialized vocabulary, in written form, made full use of all of the different scripts used in Japanese: *katakana*, *hiragana*, *kanji* and *romaji* (Roman letters).

Among all these various types of training, the most difficult was the interception of Japanese broadcasts and the translation of military telegraph messages. This kind of work, which required simultaneous translating while listening to a broadcast through earphones, was extremely taxing, as was the work of translating military telegraph messages written in *romaji*. We carried out this communications training by listening repeatedly to Japanese broadcasts recorded on phonograph records.

The teachers at this school were lower-ranking non-commissioned officers—staff sergeants and sergeants—from the second-generation Japanese-American communities in Hawaii, or from the west-coast states of California, Oregon, and Washington.

There was not a single university professor or female teacher like we had at the University of Michigan.

As for the atmosphere of this school, I don't think it was very good in comparison with what we had had at the Army Intensive Japanese Language School. One reason was that these second-generation Japanese teachers were not that interested in teaching. Born and raised in America, they wanted to prove that they were fine American citizens by demonstrating their valor on the battlefield as soldiers. Accordingly, they had nothing of the burning enthusiasm for Japanese teaching that had inspired our teachers at Michigan, for whom this teaching work had been their ticket out of the internment camps and to becoming "free men." The non-commissioned teachers at Ft. Snelling had simply been compelled to teach Japanese because they happened to have Japanese blood. Therefore, they did not really throw themselves into being teachers of Japanese, and compared with first-generation Japanese or those who had returned from a period of study in Japan, their mastery of Japanese could hardly be said to be perfect.

Secondly, we were receiving education to become commissioned officers, and these teachers, who were stuck in the ranks of low-ranking non-commissioned officers, did not have a very good feeling toward us. At least they were unable to establish the kind of warm and open relationship with us that the teachers in the Army Intensive Japanese Language School had.

In addition, a lot of rumors went around at this school, and each of them irritated us considerably. Rumors that all of us would not be able to become officers, and that those of the lowest class, whose Japanese was not very good, would not be able to become officers caused a lot of unease among us, considering that we had all worked long and hard to become officers.

Another rumor regarded investigations into our background. It was said that before one could become an army intelligence officer, the FBI had to check into one's personal history, one's ideas, one's family relationships, and so on. This made those among us who had been members of "left-wing movements" like labor unions before the war, or in some way connected with such movements, very nervous. It is apparent that these rumors were true up to a point from the fact that a fellow student who was thought to have sympathies with Communism was never able to become an officer. As indicated in the saying "where there's smoke, there's fire," even though the rumors were not true at their face value, there was an aspect of them that was true.

Moreover, there were suicides at Fort Snelling. In the midst of the pressure of studies and competition reminiscent of contemporary Japan's terrible "examination hell," classmates committed suicide by hanging themselves in the same building where I was living. These events, combined with other things like the rumors I just mentioned, gave us a great shock and put us in a pretty black mood.

Yet though unhappy things came upon us one after another, the environment at Fort Snelling in certain ways was fantastic. This was because on days off we could take a streetcar to the nearby city of Minneapolis-St. Paul and use the University of Minnesota library or student center for "intellectual activities," or have great meals in the city's restaurants. You see, most of the male students at the university had gone off to the war, leaving only the girls, so you can imagine what sort of welcome we men received.

In February 1945, I graduated from the Military Intelligence Service Language School and was commissioned as a second lieutenant. With that, I moved out of the Fort Snelling barracks, rented an apartment in Minneapolis, and started commuting to work every day by streetcar. After graduation and commissioning, our duties and place of assignment were still not confirmed, so we were ordered to wait in Minneapolis. The time spent awaiting assignment and living in my own apartment was a period of considerable freedom for me. I used the free time to visit friends, go to meals in restaurants, go drinking, and see movies. Of course, I was extremely lucky to be able to live this kind of life while the war intensified in so many parts of the world.

In April 1945, President Roosevelt passed away. I heard the news while I was still awaiting assignment in Minneapolis. Everyone was profoundly shocked and deeply saddened. Then, in June, I was sent to Pittsburg, California (a port town on the California coast near San Francisco). After receiving further training there, I waited to be sent overseas.

5

To the Front Lines in the Philippines

I LEFT PITTSBURG by ship in June, 1945, heading for a secret destination. There was an army transport ship named the *General Sherman*, which we boarded with our backpacks full of dictionaries. The ship followed a zigzag course in order to avoid submarine attack from the Japanese navy, and at night our use of lights was strictly controlled in order to prevent light from shining beyond the ship.

There was a rumor that someone caught sight of a Japanese submarine, but this was nothing more than a rumor, and our voyage was without incident. With nothing to do, I passed the time enjoying the excellent meals and taking sunbaths in the Pacific sun on deck every day. We also filled the time by playing cards every day and every night, and it was during this voyage that I learned how to play bridge.

The *U.S.S. General Sherman* continued its lone voyage, without joining a convoy, for twenty days before we arrived at the island of Ulithi, situated north of Yap Island in the western Caroline Islands. The Caroline Islands were a mandate of Japan before the war, and there had been a Japanese naval base there, but they had been occupied by the U.S. in June 1945. As one can surmise from the fact that there had been a naval base there, Ulithi was surrounded by a great coral atoll, and between the atoll and the island there were tranquil coral lakes.

However, at the time we arrived there in June, because the American occupation had just begun, the islands were still in a sorry state of destruction due to artillery bombardment, and there was not even one building that remained intact. I think there was nothing but a facility on the beach where you could drink Coca Cola. At any rate, though this was the condition Ulithi was in when we landed, we took eagerly to the short respite from shipboard living and enjoyed ourselves swimming in the sea, to the point that we forgot the passing time. Then we joined a convoy to the west of Ulithi and set out to sea again. Only when we left Ulithi did we find out that our final destination was Manila in the Philippines.

We arrived in Manila in July. My first impression of Manila right after landing was of the extensive destruction that had been caused by the fierce battles between the Japanese and American armies and the all-out war of resistance carried out by the Japanese. Almost all the buildings had been turned into mountains of rubble. It was at the beginning of February 1945 that the Sixth Army, under General Douglas MacArthur, had landed at Lingayen Bay in northern Luzon and stormed into Manila. The Japanese garrison defending Manila shut themselves up in the buildings of the city, turned the windows into rifle holes, and resisted fiercely. Even after they were overcome by the U.S. forces, while retreating they used scorched-earth tactics and resisted to the last man, making suicide attacks rather than surrendering. The battle was not over until the end of February.

As I mentioned, it was July when we landed in Manila and found it so filled with the fresh scars of warfare. Needless to say, I was shocked at the terrible scene left by the Japanese military's scorched-earth tactics. It was three-and-a-half years since I had entered the army. What war meant to me was what one heard on the radio and what one saw in the newsreels, and occupied Manila was the first time I actually witnessed a battleground. Really, no matter how much one searched in the city, one could not find a building that was intact. And as for the Filipinos, they had lost everything due to the plundering of the Japanese military during their occupation. On top of this came the battle between the Japanese and the Americans, which drove the Filipinos to near starvation.

In spite of this, however, the Filipinos welcomed the Americans like God welcoming a saint. Even though we had destroyed their daily life and imposed much suffering upon them, the Filipinos were extremely friendly and warm toward us. And I don't think this was just a momentary impression of mine, since that was still their attitude to us a year before they became an independent country. Accordingly, in July 1945, there were not that many Filipinos who desired independence from the U.S.

Anyway, without a moment's delay we began our life in the midst of this war-torn city. Even though the Japanese army had been driven from Manila, the Japanese were still putting up resistance all over the Philippines.

Though most of the city had been destroyed, the grandstand in the Santa Ana race track was spared from damage because it was made of thick concrete. We set up simple tents on the race track grounds, set up a temporary office under the grandstand,

and I began my life as a member of the Allied Translator and Interpreter Section (ATIS).

ATIS made up one part of MacArthur's command headquarters, and, true to the meaning of the word "allies," it brought together officers skilled in Japanese language from Australia, New Zealand, Britain, the U.S., and other countries.

I forgot to mention that, like the army at the University of Michigan, the U.S. Navy had also set up a Japanese language training school in Boulder, Colorado, where they also educated a large number of Japanese-language officers. The Australians and the British also had Japanese-language training schools. Accordingly, I got to know and worked with a lot of language officers from the U.S. Navy's Japanese language school. So, although I began my intelligence activities in Manila as a member of a part of MacArthur's headquarters, I never once laid eyes on MacArthur himself.

ATIS brought together people of many stripes, and one I remember well was an army officer from Australia. He had been working as a Jewish rabbi in Sydney, but he learned Japanese on his own, joined the Australian army, graduated from the Japanese training school, and came to Manila as a member of ATIS.

He was the commander of the Santa Ana Japanese prisoner-of-war camp, and he was in charge of the employment of prisoners for garden construction and sidewalk maintenance service. He worked and lived together with the Japanese prisoners, and because he loved to sing, he sang all kinds of Japanese songs with them. He also had fun teaching them and leading them in singing various Jewish songs, like Hatikva ("The Hope"), now the Israeli national anthem. Even now I cannot forget this heart-warming sight, but unfortunately I cannot remember his real name. The Japanese prisoners called him *otoosan* (father), and we affectionately called him "Holy Joe," but as for his real name. . . .

The war situation in Luzon at the time was overwhelmingly in favor of the allied forces. Before the transport ships arrived from Japan, they were sunk by U.S. navy planes or submarines, and even if one made it to Luzon, its passengers would be driven into the mountainous jungle, from where they could put up very little real resistance.

Accordingly, in line with the military's motto of "Put things in order quickly and then stand by," we kept up with our standby posture, passing the time by reading, playing bridge, and talking to the Filipinos.

"You are needed for the interrogation of some newly arrived prisoners." This request, I believe, came during the time that we were on standby.

Generally speaking, through this period of the war, we had great difficulty getting any Japanese prisoners, who were an extremely precious source of information. For one thing, the American soldiers usually preferred to shoot Japanese soldiers rather than take them as prisoners. And really, it was probably unreasonable to ask the U.S. soldiers to take live prisoners under the extremely harsh conditions of jungle warfare. In addition, the Field Service Code of the Japanese military declared "One does not endure the shame of being taken alive as a prisoner," and the soldiers had an extreme aversion to being captured, often choosing death instead.

For these reasons, either because they were totally dispirited or because they had lost their physical freedom, if they did happen to get taken prisoner, they fell into despair and told us everything without reserve. What they said included a lot of extremely valuable information.

In contrast, the American soldiers had all been thoroughly trained that, "If you are captured, you answer with your name, rank, and serial number, and nothing else."

Even if the principle was "Do not endure the shame of being captured alive," by July of 1945, the Japanese were already being pursued by the U.S. army and the Philippine guerrillas, and they had been driven into a small area deep in the mountains of Luzon Island. Without weapons or ammunition, without food or clothing, they were just wandering aimlessly in the jungle. So though we were still not getting many prisoners, the number was gradually increasing.

Even though the battle for the Philippines had already been won by the Americans, we still wanted information from the Japanese prisoners. This was because, while there was little doubt that in the battle for Okinawa we would also be victorious, the next operation—the "Operation Olympic," a landing on the Japanese mainland—was already being planned and prepared for, and for that purpose it was crucial to gather information about conditions within Japan.

The Japanese reinforcement troops sent to the Philippines were reservists who had not received very much training, but most of them had left Japan just a few months earlier, so if they were skillfully questioned, one could obtain the latest information about circumstances in Japan.

I conducted the interrogation of some Japanese prisoners. The place where we did the interrogation was a small wooden hut with an earthen floor, a dark room with almost no windows. The Japanese prisoners were brought into this dark room stark naked, then they would suddenly have a spotlight shone on them and the interrogation would begin from a place high above them. The interrogation desk must have been elevated some ten feet above the floor.

I have no idea who came up with this stage design, but it was remarkably effective. All the prisoners had been fed propaganda to the effect that if they were captured by the Americans they would be killed, and when this was added to their weakened physical and mental condition, due to wandering exhausted and sick in the jungle, most of them gave up all resistance and answered the interrogation honestly.

They told us a lot of things—about how their homes had been destroyed in American air raids, about how many people had been killed, about how their homes had been burned down by fire, about their family members left behind in their native towns, about their wives and children, and so on.

We asked them what sort of movies were being shown currently in Tokyo. This was because we could make certain inferences about the living situation of ordinary people if we knew whether or not people were able to go to the movies. The answer, in most cases, was that it was possible to go. That is, it seemed that they enjoyed going to the movies, and they talked to us about the movies that they had seen.

I was totally devoted to my role as a language officer, and I limited my work to translating and interpreting Japanese, but I think that at least the Japanese prisoners felt no incongruity about the fact that I was interrogating them in Japanese, and they answered me submissively. I think this was the fruit of my over two years of Japanese language training, and it demonstrated the value of the "special training" I had received at the University of Michigan and Fort Snelling.

I was able to interrogate the prisoners in very fluent Japanese, and I myself also felt reasonably comfortable in the vernacular of the time. For example, when I asked the prisoners about the movies being shown in Tokyo, I did not use the current word *eiga* for "movie," but the word that the Japanese usually used at the time, "moving pictures," or literally, "moving photographs" (*katsudo shashin*).

Actually, however, for me this was my first experience of

interrogating Japanese people in Japanese. Of course, excluding my conversations with the first- and second-generation Japanese and Japanese-born Americans who had taught us the language, I had had a few very simple conversations with Japanese POWs engaged in labor service, but these were not occasions that one could really call "work." The interrogations, on the other hand, were the first real work that I had done as an intelligence officer. For that reason, I was extremely concerned about whether the prisoners would actually understand my Japanese, but in the end it all went very well.

During this period—six weeks from the beginning of July to the end of the war on August 15th—there were as many as three practice attempts to mount "Operation Olympic," to invade the Japanese mainland. Each time I stuffed all my clothes, provisions, and dictionaries into my backpack, and we headed en masse for Manila harbor, where we boarded the waiting transport ships. No one who has not experienced this sort of mass boarding can imagine how difficult it is. In addition to all of the ordinary equipment, we translators had to stuff several huge dictionaries into our backpacks, like Meiseisha's *Kan'Ei Jiten* (Kanji-English Dictionary) and Kenkyusha's *Shin Wa-Ei Daijiten* (New Japanese-English Dictionary), and then, with all this on our backs, we had to climb up on nets from the launch boats and crawl on hands and knees into the transport ships. If the backpacks were too heavy, we would get stuck halfway up the nets, and when this happened we had to have the soldiers climbing up behind us help us by pushing us from behind. Although we joked with our fellow soldiers that these thick dictionaries would make great bullet shields during the landing operation in Kyushu, even now I can't forget how heavy they were.

"Operation Olympic" was practiced three times, as I said, and each time it was called off, but frankly speaking I don't really know why. Perhaps it was simply a sort of exercise, or perhaps the policy was changed in midstream, or maybe it was a combination of both. I can only say one thing for sure. If this "Operation Olympic" had gone ahead, an inconceivable number of Japanese soldiers, Japanese civilians, and American soldiers would have been killed and wounded.

In the battle of Iwo Jima, 6,000 American soldiers and 21,000 Japanese soldiers were killed. In Okinawa 12,000 Americans and 110,000 Japanese died, including civilians. If "Operation Olympic" had been carried out, the number of Japanese and American casualties would certainly have exceeded these numbers by ten or fifteen times or more. Even though the Japanese "mainland" consists of islands, their size and population cannot be compared with Iwo Jima and Okinawa.

We heard the news about the atomic bombs dropped in Hiroshima and Nagasaki in early August 1945, when the preparations for "Operation Olympic" were still underway. As is well known now, in July 1945, in Alamagordo, New Mexico, the first atomic bomb test in history was successfully carried out. The success of the test was immediately conveyed to President Truman. The two bombs that had already been completed were then loaded onto cruisers for the purpose of being used in the Pacific theater, and they were transported to Tinian Island, just south of Saipan. It was on August 6th that a B-29 took off from Tinian Island and dropped the first bomb on Hiroshima. Then on the 9th the second bomb was dropped on Nagasaki.

My honest impression when I heard the news about the atomic bombs was the thought: "Now the war is over!" I was pleased and encouraged. But I must say that at that time I had no knowledge of the atomic bomb's horrible destructive power. I simply felt that this "secret weapon" would force the Japanese to surrender more quickly and make "Operation Olympic" unnecessary, minimizing the sacrifices that we would have to make.

On August 15th came the total surrender of the Japanese military. A long war was finally over. I spent that day in Manila, but I will never forget the feelings I had at the time. On that day we drove around the streets of Manila in our jeeps blowing whistles, waving the Stars and Stripes and calling out to the people walking by, "We won! We won!" The Filipinos shared the joy of victory with us.

6

Meeting the Surrender Envoys

ON AUGUST 19TH, 1945, a surrender mission consisting of sixteen Japanese leaders headed by Vice Admiral Kawabe Torashi arrived in Manila, and we suddenly found ourselves very busy. With Japan's surrender, MacArthur's headquarters had to quickly switch from preparing for a landing operation to preparing for the occupation of Japan, and for this purpose he ordered that Japanese government representatives be sent to Manila. According to the instructions of MacArthur's headquarters, the envoys first flew to Ieshima, near Okinawa, aboard white-painted aircraft with green crosses on the sides of the fuselage and on the wings for identification. Then they flew to Manila aboard American military aircraft.

We were quickly called together at the ATIS office at the Santa Ana racetrack, and then ordered to translate immediately a vast quantity of Japanese documents that had been provided by the Japanese envoys. It was necessary to carry out the translation both quickly and accurately. The Japanese envoys were waiting in Manila, and MacArthur's headquarters needed the translations before conferring with them as the basis for giving them instructions about the policies that would be enacted. So we split up the work among the members of the team and managed to translate this vast quantity of documents in 48 hours straight through.

The materials that we translated dealt with the Japanese military forces that, at the time of the defeat, were deployed in New Guinea, Singapore, and all other Pacific locations, as well as the military forces dispersed or deployed in continental China. Concretely, they gave the quantity of military personnel, weapons, ammunition, and air power deployed in the region, and information regarding Japanese naval vessels cruising in the area. Of course, I participated in this translation work, and stayed up all night to get it done. If I exclude the interpretation I had done in the interrogation of prisoners mentioned above, which was not really pure translation, this was the true beginning of my work as a translator.

I felt that this was meaningful work, because it allowed me to play a part, in whatever small way I could, in the conclusion of the war. And frankly, while the documents provided by the Japanese side were accurate and detailed, I think our translation work was no less valuable for its promptness and accuracy.

The translation itself consisted mainly of statistical data, so the content was not all that difficult, but to do it all in the limited time allowed us required quite a high level of translation ability. In addition to the "special training" we had received at the University of Michigan and Fort Snelling, we had also built up the abilities required for the job by the actual war theater training we had received at the front in the Philippines.

The staff of MacArthur's headquarters left Manila in advance by plane in order to attend the surrender signing ceremony to be held aboard the *U.S.S. Missouri*, and the vanguard group arrived at Atsugi Airport on August 28. We followed them later, leaving Manila by ship and arriving in the port of Yokohama on October 1. The voyage from Manila to Yokohama was as peaceful as one could imagine, because there was no need to follow a zigzag course to avoid Japanese submarines. With this the members of ATIS all withdrew from the office at the Santa Ana racetrack and relocated to the NYK Building in central Tokyo.

Our Landing in Japan

I FIRST SET EYES on Japan from the troop ship as we entered Yokohama Harbor, October 1, 1945. Nothing much remained of the city but scorched earth due to the total destruction from aerial bombing, and it was a pathetic sight. And it was not just Yokohama—every building and facility in the urban/industrial belt from distant Kawasaki to Tokyo had been destroyed by bombing. I still remember how shocked I felt to see that, except for a few remaining protrusions from two or three buildings like the American Consulate, near Yokohama Harbor, everything had been completely flattened. How could a country so totally destroyed have continued to fight a war with America?

Since the docking facilities had also been destroyed, we landed at Yokohama using landing craft. After landing, we were transported from Yokohama to Tokyo in army trucks, and the first lodging we were able to settle down in was the YWCA Building at Ochanomizu, where two officers were billeted in

36

each room. After about two weeks there, we were relocated to the Nippon Yusen Kaisha Building in Marunouchi, which was known by the abbreviation NYK. The YWCA was cramped and had only enough space for lodging, so we spent two weeks in a standby condition, unable to work, until we could move to the NYK, where we could get hold of some office space.

As is probably clear if one looks at photographs taken at the time, near the NYK Building, buildings such as the Daiichi Seimei Building, the Meiji Seimei Building, the Kaijo Building, the Marunouchi Building, and the Imperial Hotel were still standing, and although Tokyo Station had been partially destroyed, half of it was still functional. It was these buildings that had survived the fires. I think that a few of these buildings were still being used—in their original form—in the period of rapid economic growth in the 1960s.

Incidentally, the reason that these buildings remained, although Tokyo had been turned into a desolate burned-out wasteland, was that they were built of steel-reinforced concrete, which was resistant against attack by incendiary bombs, and moreover, because they had been purposely excluded as bombing targets in order that they could be used by the American forces after the country was occupied.

Though the U.S. military turned Tokyo into a veritable wasteland, at the same time, after it became clear how the war would end, they began to leave certain buildings intact through precision bombing. The result of this policy was, I think, something remarkable to the point that one could call it a miracle.

For instance, a good example was the Daiichi Hotel. The Marunouchi and Shimbashi districts were very small corners of Tokyo, but the Daiichi Hotel was spared from bombing, while everything else from the neighboring street to Shinbashi Station was completely flattened. Even though this Daiichi Hotel was supposed to have opened in Tokyo in 1940, its construction had to be suspended due to the outbreak of war in Europe. It was the newest hotel in Tokyo, built for the then-anticipated 1940 Olympics.

So every one of the buildings that had been removed from the list of bombing targets was allocated to the use of the occupying army's officers and men. The most typical, no doubt, was the Daiichi Seimei Building where MacArthur's General Headquarters was located.

The building allocated to us with ATIS was the NYK Building. On floors one to three of this building, which had one floor underground and seven floors above ground, were the ATIS offices. The fourth floor was used for the officers' billet, and the fifth to the seventh floors for the non-commissioned officers' billets. Only the basement was permitted to be used by the owners, NYK. As for myself, I lodged on the fourth floor, went down to the ground floor office to work, and went back to the fourth floor to sleep. This was my daily routine—there could hardly have been anything more convenient.

Of course, this is not to say that I never set foot outside the NYK Building. On the contrary. Whenever I had any free time I did my best to go out into the town and talk to Japanese people. For a guy who had received over two years of Japanese training in school and at the battlefront, to be able to talk in this way to ordinary Japanese people was something unbelievably interesting. It meant being able to use Japanese on its real home ground—Japan itself. Of course, I had had the experience of interrogating prisoners, but that was only one time, and it was only under the special circumstances of war.

To state in a few words my impressions of the Japanese at the time, it was that they were extremely poor and unclean, as well as very skinny and feeble-looking. The women wore ragged

Japanese-style pantaloons gathered at the ankles. The men wore ragged military uniforms. They wore strange-looking hats and strange-looking spectacles, and their yellowed teeth flashed forth when they spoke. Food rations were in terribly short supply, and they were eating almost nothing but white radishes (*daikon*), onions, and squashes. Moreover, soap was in short supply, and the Japanese were rarely able to take baths. For these reasons, I think, when they spoke, the air they exhaled had a foul smell, not to mention their very pungent body odor.

In spite of all this, I remember that I was bewildered at their so-called "craze for English." Though I would address them in Japanese, almost no one would answer me in Japanese. They all answered in English!

Subsequently, I had many chances to visit Japan, and even now, if I address someone in Japanese in Tokyo, if they judge from my face that I am a foreigner (a *gaijin*), they will answer in English instead of Japanese. It seems that Japanese people tend to think automatically that *gaijin* are Americans, and thus they assume without a second thought that they should speak to them in English.

Since the vast majority of the *gaijin* who came to Japan right after the defeat *were* American officers and soldiers, it was not that unnatural that *gaijin* should come to be synonymous with "American," but even so I was somewhat bewildered by the fact that they would speak to us in English.

Just a few months earlier hadn't they detested English as the language of the enemy, hesitating to utter even one word, and referred to the English speakers as "those brutish Yanks and Brits"? Now, because of the defeat, they made a 180-degree turnabout, speaking to us in English and even refusing to answer in Japanese to those "strange *gaijin*" (*hen na gaijin*) who were able to speak their language.

Kids would come up to us and yell, "Hello, Joe!," "Give me some chewing gum!," "Give me candy!" and so on, and adults, being adults, would eagerly, or courageously, come up and say to us, "Wat iz democrasie?" or "Wat shudo uwe du abouto de Emperor?" They really showered us with questions about this sort of important problem. And of course, in English: "Can we come to your room?" "Can you come home with us?"

I suppose it was because they wanted to practice more English conversation that they wanted to visit our rooms, or invite us to visit their homes. However, we were not able to invite them to our quarters, but the opposite was also prohibited by GHQ. There was one reason for this. It was because the policy of GHQ SCAP was that we must not cause any worsening of the food shortage and fuel shortages that Japan was suffering immediately after the end of the war. Therefore, we could not accept any invitations from Japanese people. Anyway, we were living in the NYK Building, using it both for billets and offices. But the greatest defect of this building was that it had no heating.

We moved into the NYK Building at the end of October, not far from the season when heating would become necessary, but the heating equipment had been removed for scrap iron due to the wartime requisition policy. A hole for a steam pipe remained uselessly in the wall, but the heating apparatus itself was nowhere to be found.

So on the orders of my superior, I went down to the basement and ordered the president of NYK to have the heating apparatus installed immediately. However, the president replied that it was not possible to install it because it had been removed for scrap iron due to wartime requisition. So I said to him in a loud voice, "You find me that heating equipment! This is an order from General MacArthur!"

We gave them some jeeps, and together we drove all around Tokyo for several days. And would you believe it? The heating apparatus that had been removed from the NYK Building was found discarded in the open in a scrap pile, still intact! Once we discovered it, we immediately had it moved by truck to the NYK Building and installed. As a result, though the first winter in Tokyo after the end of the war was a severe one, it was a warm and comfortable time for those of us working in the NYK Building.

All the same, in this single incident regarding the heating apparatus, I think that the signs of the terminal state of Japan's war economy are thrown into high relief. The American military had set up a maritime blockade around Japan. Within the country, we were carrying out carpet bombing. The labor force was shattered, the machinery had been largely destroyed, and in a situation where everything was in short supply, precious resources that had been requisitioned in desperation and in urgent need lay discarded in a scrap heap, fulfilling no function whatever.

In this case, with the one *ex cathedra* statement, "By the order of General MacArthur!" we had been able to get back the heating apparatus. Let me mention one more case where we managed to accomplish a strange "job" using exactly the same tactic.

I think it was about October 1945. The order came from the supreme commander of the Daiichi Seimei Building, General MacArthur, to "find me a chair!" When we asked why, we were told that he had set up an office in the president's office of the Daiichi Seimei Building and did not like the chair that was already in the office, so he wanted us to find him another one. Thus, I ended up having to go on a chair hunt with two or three of my subordinate non-commissioned officers.

"So where in the world should we go to look for a chair?", we thought. We walked around one by one to all the remaining buildings that could still be called buildings in the Marunouchi area, and all the remaining offices that could still be called offices. We finally ended up at the Meiji Seimei Building, which was not all that far from the NYK Building, or from the Daiichi Seimei Building. I asked for directions to the president's office, walked right in, and said to the president, who was engrossed in his work, "Please show me your chair."

He looked at me as I entered his office and listened to my words, and for a moment he appeared totally bewildered. Then he apparently judged that it must be an American officer who had entered his office.

The expression on his face said clearly, "*Why do you want my chair?*"

I looked carefully at the chair, and I immediately concluded that it was a superb chair that even MacArthur would certainly be satisfied with. Without making any attempt to cajole the president, I ordered my subordinates who were waiting outside the room to come in and carry out the chair. To the president, who was standing erect in astonishment by my side, I said,

"Give me a piece of paper, please."

I wrote a note to the effect that a chair that had been in use in the president's room of the Meiji Seimei Building had been requisitioned by General MacArthur. I added the date, signed MacArthur's signature myself, and handed the piece of paper back to the president. Then in a solemn voice I proclaimed,

"I hereby requisition your chair. It is the order of General MacArthur!"

Needless to say, the president of Meiji Seimei obeyed my words without a murmur. So we carried the chair to the Daiichi Seimei Building. Whether Macarthur was satisfied with it or not, or what later became of the chair, I have no idea. But I think it was a chair worthy of a man in MacArthur's position, and I hope that it served his needs quite well.

I must make it clear, however, that this was something that happened under the Occupation, and that under the terms of the Occupation the Japanese were obliged to supply the Occupation army with whatever they needed. Thus, if one thinks about it, perhaps this sort of thing was really unavoidable. At any rate, we took care of the various things that had to be done, and before long the ATIS office had been set up in the NYK Building and commenced full-scale operation.

8

My Work as an ATIS Officer

ONE OF THE MAIN JOBS OF ATIS was to translate Japanese daily newspapers like the *Yomiuri* and the *Mainichi* and deliver our translations by the next morning to MacArthur's GHQ. In the morning, MacArthur was thus able to read about the various events reported in the previous day's newspaper in English without the slightest inconvenience.

This work was carried out by the members of ATIS, but it was too much for us to do on our own. So we decided to hire Japanese who were good at English. We planned to hire a hundred Japanese, and they had to be capable of reading, writing, and translating English. My work was to carry out the employment examination interviews. So I put an employment ad in the newspapers seeking qualified individuals.

A really large number of people responded. It was quite an impressive sight: there were the elderly and the young, men and women. I think that everyone who had confidence in his or her

English abilities responded to the ad. From all these applicants, we had to choose those who were the most excellent. Among those that we hired, there were old gentlemen who had graduated from universities like Princeton or Harvard before the war, and women who said they had graduated from famous women's universities like Bryn Mawr or Smith.

In addition, there were women and men of mixed American and Japanese blood who had been unable to return to the U.S. at the outbreak of hostilities and had to stay in Japan against their will. There were first- and second-generation Japanese-Americans, naturalized Americans of Japanese descent, and Filipinos, Thais, Indians, and other Asians who had had no choice but to stay in Japan through the war.

Among those we hired there was even a Brazilian of Japanese descent. Although his native language, of course, was Portuguese, his English was extremely good. Without the slightest hesitation we added his name to the list of those to be hired. Among the people I hired, as noted earlier, there were also some women who had graduated from American universities before the war and returned to Japan to get married, who had no experience of going out to work until this recruitment. If they were Japanese women who graduated from American universities before the war, they were almost all prim young ladies from upper-class families, and very few of them had ever worked after getting married. Yet at this time they could no longer rely on their upper-class background. They had either lost their homes in the air raids or lost their husbands in the war, so that they had no family or property to rely on and had to find a job after the defeat just to have enough food to eat.

In this period from 1945 to 1946, a job connected with the Occupation army was the best thing anyone who was looking for work could hope for. Accordingly, especially in the case of women, they appeared at the interview examination in their very best clothes. They wore beautiful kimonos that they must have guarded with their lives at the time of the air raids and during the food crisis after the defeat, and they had their hair done up beautifully. And they bowed their elegantly coiffured heads low before us and begged us politely, "Please give me a job."

Because we had far more applicants than we expected, I think it took us two weeks just to conduct the interviews, even though we carried out interviews all day long one after another. After that came the translation tests. In this way, we finally managed to hire almost a hundred translators. We gave them what at the time was an extraordinarily good wage, but I think that it pleased them even more that we provided them with food. When they worked overtime, we gave them beef and pork over and above their wages, and prepared lunch for them, and this was surely more important to them than their wages. This suggests just how bad the food shortage was in the period right after the end of the war.

We divided the hundred employees into a daytime shift and a night shift, and carried on the translation work twenty-four hours a day. Each of the Japanese employees had a desk in a large room on the first floor of the NYK Building, and they commenced their translation work under our supervision.

Incidentally, the large room in which we carried out this newspaper translation work was on the left-hand side of the ground floor of the NYK Building, if viewed from the front, while on the right-hand side was the room for translating the various materials regarding residences, food provisions, and so on that were sent to us from MacArthur's GHQ. In a corner on the right-hand side was also a room where we translated the many letters that MacArthur received from Japanese people, as have been fully discussed in Rinjiro Sodei's book *Dear General*

MacArthur: Letters from the Japanese during the American Occupation (Lanham, Md.: Rowan & Littlefield Publishers, 2001).

As for myself, at the time when we commenced the full-scale newspaper translation work with our Japanese employees, that is, in November 1945, I received an order transferring me from the newspaper translation room to the room for translating the letters written to MacArthur. Therefore, although I had made all the arrangements for the newspaper translation work, I was transferred out before I ever had a chance to really get involved.

However, since this transfer was just a matter of moving from the left to the right side of the NYK Building, it was nothing like the kind of work transfer that is frequently experienced by Japanese salarymen in Japan. Moreover, since I was still living in the same building, there was no change in my living situation.

My routine after moving into the NYK Building was: breakfast at 7:00, commence work on the first floor of the same building at 8:00, work until noon, go up to the fourth floor for lunch, and then work in the afternoon back on the first floor until 5:00. After 5:00 I would have dinner and drinks in the officers' club on the fourth floor. Whatever I did, I just went up and down the elevator in the same building every day.

Moreover, when I first moved into the NYK Building, I did not often go outside. If I did, it was not like there were buses, and we couldn't even use taxis to get around. We had the jeeps that we always used, but to drive through Tokyo when almost all of the street lights had been destroyed was an extremely dangerous matter. From the first evening, even if we went out, there was almost nothing to be seen, and what is more, because it was a time of extreme food shortages, there were not even Japanese restaurants in which to enjoy ourselves. In a word, Tokyo was a "dead city."

So normally we spent our evenings in the officers' club in the

NYK Building. Here we were able to enjoy American movies every night, and because there were frequent parties, we were certainly not bored. On the contrary, we were privileged to be able to eat good food and drink good alcohol, passing our time playing cards and chatting.

It was about the end of the year, after I had spent nearly three months living in the NYK Building, before I finally got fed up with this life and managed to get away from Tokyo.

On the weekends, we went, for example, to the Izu Peninsula or Hakone and enjoyed a taste of country life and hot springs in Japan. Of course, we took along our own food. GHQ had ordered that if we went on a trip, we had to take along our C-rations, which were our provisions for field warfare. The reason, as I mentioned earlier, was that it was the policy of the Occupation army not to aggravate the burden on the Japanese people caused by the extreme shortage of food.

I went many times to hot springs at places like Miyanoshita in Hakone or Shuzenji in Izu, and among them, I have wonderful memories of the Fujiya Hotel in Miyanoshita. From before the war this hotel was famous for its extremely gorgeous dining room, and, in addition, it had a large number of beautiful and luxurious rooms with brightly polished *tokonoma* alcoves. It was here that we stayed.

We had come with our C-rations, and we traded these to the Japanese for fresh eggs, milk, and vegetables. The C-rations really came in handy, not only because they were hard to come by, but because they contained highly nutritious food in the right balance, so the Japanese regarded them as precious things, gladly trading whatever we wanted for them.

In this way, when the weekends came, I would take along four or five of my buddies and go out to the hot springs. The trains that we used were always crowded and dirty. However, the Japanese from the country who were over fifty were extremely friendly, and they would often offer us their seats.

Sometime after the beginning of the occupation there appeared special trains for the exclusive use of the Occupation army soldiers, but there was no such thing at the end of 1945, or, even if there were a few, their number was very limited and they were not available for immediate use. Thus to go out to places like Izu and Hakone we used the same trains that the Japanese used.

This was an extremely interesting experience, since it gave us a glimpse into the lives of the Japanese people at that time. The trains were full of Japanese who were on food-hunting expeditions, carrying big packages on their backs. Most of them were city dwellers, and they were hurrying back home after having taken whatever small amounts of clothing they had left after the air raids, and their rings and jewelry, to the countryside to trade for food items like rice and pumpkins. Here we get another image of just how severe the food shortage was.

Compared to this desperate condition of the city dwellers, the country people that we met on our weekend sojourns in Izu or Hakone were pure of heart and simple. Moreover, the damage from air raids was much less in the country, so the influence of the war was lighter and the food supplies were relatively plentiful.

For this reason, the countryside was a very healthful place to be. The children had mucous running out of both nostrils, but they ran and jumped around healthily and looked totally different from the sickly children of the city.

What is more, the country people were very approachable, and they seemed to have a great interest in us. They were not particularly surprised if we addressed them in Japanese, and they never answered in English like the people in the city. It seemed as though they thought that it was completely natural that *gaijin* spoke Japanese, and that the whole world spoke Japanese.

However, they were very interested in our physiques and in our clothing, and they came to peek in when we were taking a bath. It was a little disconcerting when they put their hands on the pockets of our clothing and wanted to see what was inside, but. . . .

In the midst of this I had a strange experience. I mentioned that we would exchange our C-rations for eggs, milk, vegetables and so on. When we encountered an item of food that we had never seen before, we would ask "What is this?"

Yet the response that came to us from the country people was, "Ha, ha, ha, ha, ha. Ha, ha, ha, ha!"

I gradually began to understand that at such times Japanese absolutely do not ask "What is this?", even if they do not know what the item is. An American would surely respond to such a question without laughing, saying, for instance, "This is a turnip, this is sea urchin, this is octopus, and that is quail."

At first I thought that this sort of behavior was only characteristic of country folk, and moreover that it reflected the loss of Japanese self-confidence immediately following the defeat, but recently I have begun to think that such is not the case. For, about two years ago, I invited an American friend who had never been to Japan to go with me to a traditional Japanese-style inn in Shuzenji in Izu where I had stayed several times in the early days of the Occupation. At dinner time, as is common in Japanese inns, a waitress set up a table in our room, brought the food into the room, and arranged a wide variety of about fifteen different types of side dishes on small plates.

Because this was my friend's first time in Japan, he was extremely interested in what these side dishes were, and he asked me, "What is this?" I also did not know what some of the dishes laid on the plates were, so I asked the waitress in Japanese, "What is this?" Her response was again to break out laughing, and that was the only reply I got. I asked about this later, and it appears that this waitress herself did not know what the dishes were.

Whether that was the case or not, it seems that to ask about the contents of a meal that has been served is not regarded as very good manners in Japan. Moreover, if we go to a restaurant and we don't like the seats we are given, we clearly state the reason and ask for a different seat: "Excuse me, but the music is loud here, so please let us change to this seat over here." Or "Pardon me, but the air conditioning is too cold here. Please let us change to that seat over there." In Japan there are very few people who would speak so directly.

Perhaps one could say that we live in a culture that tells us not to trust other people completely, or in which a somewhat troublesome procedure is deemed necessary before we can trust them. The Japanese, on the other hand, begin speaking from the silent premise of 100% trust. Unexpectedly, it seems that the differences between American and Japanese culture reveal themselves clearly even in little things like the manners one follows in eating meals.

9

Letters to General MacArthur

IT WAS IN NOVEMBER 1945 that I moved from the big room on the left side of the NYK Building to the room on the right, i.e., from the newspaper translation department to the department for translating letters sent to General MacArthur.

Since, as mentioned above, Rinjiro Sodei has already introduced and analyzed the content of the love letters and fan letters that General MacArthur received from Japanese people beginning right after the end of the war, I will discuss them from the point of view of an officer responsible for translating them into English.

The head of this department was Major John Shelton of the Australian army. He was the son of a white Russian father and a Japanese mother, and he had Australian citizenship. There were about ten of us responsible for translation, mostly American officers and including non-commissioned officers who were second-generation Japanese.

I remember not only that MacArthur was addressed with all kinds of nicknames, but also that the addresses to which the letters were sent were various and sundry. Some people wrote "Tokyo, General Ma." Some wrote "Japan, General Ma." And some wrote "Tokyo Daiichi Seimei Building, General MacArthur." In many cases, the addresses were very abbreviated. There was even a letter that managed to reach us which was just addressed to "General MacArthur."

At the time every person in Japan knew the name of General MacArthur, and because it was also well known that his office was in the Daiichi Seimei Building, even the most simply addressed letter would reach us. Though letters to MacArthur had started to arrive from very early in the Occupation, at the time when I was involved, namely around the end of 1945, he would receive between ten and forty letters every day. And of course they varied greatly in length.

MacArthur's headquarters ordered us to translate all the letters immediately, i.e., the same day they were received. So whether ten or twenty letters came on a certain day, they all had to be translated and sent off to the GHQ staff in the Daiichi Seimei Building by 5:00 P.M. that day. And, of course, we were required to translate the letters in full, not just write a summary. Thus, no matter how stupid or ridiculous a letter was, even if it seemed that the writer must be crazy, we had to provide a complete translation.

The stationery that the writers used also came in all shapes and sizes. It was the time of shortages of everything right after the war. So one could not expect that the kind of fine quality letter-writing stationery we have today was available. Some people used the back of the envelope, and some used the back of the labels from canned foods.

If there were letters written by brush in beautiful calligraphy, there were also those written in pen or pencil. Some letters came decorated with drawings of men and women having sex. The content, like the written characters, varied greatly, from those praising MacArthur to those discussing the Emperor system, to those offering opinions, to those making requests, etc. Let me just mention a couple that I translated myself that left particularly strong impressions.

Quite a few letters divulged "secret" information to us. For instance, there was frequently information about hidden weapons or ammunition. Right before and after the end of the war, because of fear of confiscation by the U.S. military, Japanese soldiers hid weapons, ammunition, food supplies, and the like underground or in caves and other places. To find and expose these hidden caches was absolutely essential to the peacekeeping mission of the Occupation army, and in many cases it was letters to General MacArthur that provided the clues to their discovery. Our translated manuscripts were immediately turned over to the G-2 (GHQ Section 2, in charge of intelligence and peacekeeping), and troops would be sent out to find and secure the caches.

In addition, it is a bit of an exaggeration to call it "secret" information, but there were also a lot of letters that said things such as: in my town, or in my village—there is an ultranationalist, or a militarist, so I respectfully ask that he be punished. The men that were singled out for exposure were, in most cases, landlords, police officers, or schoolteachers who had played an important role during the war in that particular town or village. In the case of this type of letter as well, our translations were passed on to G-2. There were also letters that said that "there is a strange foreigner in my village," like the case of Ba Maw that I will discuss later.

These sorts of letters, needless to say, played an important role in the Occupation administration as information sources. The majority of the letters were certainly serious and written using solid and substantial language and proper form. Of course, since there were so many, there were also inevitably strange letters, but I think that they were few enough to be called exceptions.

A lot of letters were accompanied by presents for MacArthur. These included artworks, clothing, food items, photographs, and just about everything else under the sun. There were even presents for MacArthur's family. Most of these presents are now on exhibit at the MacArthur Memorial in Norfolk, Virginia. I tried to make a list of the presents on the basis of the museum's documents, but I have just provided a list of the categories in the chart on the next pages. It would probably not be an overstatement to say that they included every type of item conceivable.

There were also a great many invitations—something different from a present but which can be understood as having just about the same purpose: invitations to luncheons, invitations to dinner parties, invitations to nightclubs. Every sort of invitation one can imagine found its way to MacArthur's GHQ. There were even invitations to the opening of newly refurbished restaurants. Again, all of them were translated by us and passed on to GHQ.

Another type of letter that left a strong impression on me were the ones written by Japanese women asking for the privilege of giving birth to "My Revered and Beloved General MacArthur's" child. There were not only two or three such letters. In the less than three months that I was working in this department, just until the end of 1945, I counted eighty of them.

Gifts from the Imperial family to General MacArthur
> Model sailboat, puppy, fish, ducks, model of a Japanese
> house (the model sailboat and the puppy were presents for
> MacArthur's son Arthur)

Gifts for General MacArthur
> Pigs, apples, painting of Mt. Fuji in a fragrant-wood frame,
> persimmons, portrait of Abraham Lincoln, morning
> glories, sword made by a famous swordmaker, songbook,
> ginkgo nuts, flowers, fruits, Japanese dolls, fishing pole,
> rice, yams, lily bulbs, soybeans, scroll paintings, goldfish,
> books, pottery and porcelains, Hotei figurines, sandals, silk
> fabrics, turkeys, lacquerware, plates, oil painting, bamboo
> toys, mandarin oranges, rice cakes, raisins, poster of
> Christ, embroideries, funds for the construction of a
> bronze statue of MacArthur, birthday cake, painting of
> bamboo, deerskin and antlers, women's hair ornaments,
> potted plant, pears, silver cups, raised picture,
> photographs, poetry collections, female bird, walking
> stick, biscuits, handkerchiefs, sword-hilt ornament, knife
> attached to sword sheath, lacquered cups, antique helmet,
> stone model of Mt. Fuji, wall hangings, sword, canary,
> leather office utensils, play tools for children, bonsai, bust
> of MacArthur, ceramics, one set of tea ceremony and
> ikebana implements, Bibles, seaweed, kimonos, fans,
> bowls, badminton birds, red beans, suit of armor, wooden
> sword, masks, portrait of the Emperor Meiji, kumquat
> tree, silk curtains, cotton shirts, bear cub, medicinal
> powder, fireflies, Daruma dolls, tomatoes, chairs, tin
> products, wrapping cloths (*furoshiki*), cookies, seeds, geta
> (wooden sandles), fox furs, deerskin rug, sake, candles,
> bearskin, salmon, honey

Gifts for Mrs. MacArthur
> Silk products, chestnuts, grapes, melons, biwa, comb,
> portrait, Noritake pottery, *ukiyoe* painting, flowers, dolls,
> book on tea ceremony, earrings, kimono

"My Revered and Beloved Honorable General MacArthur. I long to receive the blessed seed of your child. I am embarrassed to impose upon you when you are so busy, but please come to my residence at the following address at XX o'clock. . . ." At first I thought that these letters must have been written by women who were a bit out of their minds, but whatever one might think of the content, to judge from the quality of the writing and context, they had to be fully possessed of their senses. Moreover, it was very clear from my experience as a translator that the letters were not being sent by the same person. All the same, it is hardly necessary to say that we burst out laughing while we were translating them. The first time I received such a letter I asked my superior, Major Shelton, "Is it OK to translate this sort of letter?"

"It doesn't matter. We have to translate everything. It is not up to us to determine the degree of importance—that's up to the bigwigs at GHQ."

General MacArthur must have been shocked when he read these letters. There is, of course, no way to know how he felt when he read the love letters that were translated, but I imagine that he was surprised. However, these letters can be seen as interesting material for inferring the psychological condition of Japanese women in the Occupation period. In comparison with the spiritually broken condition of Japanese men at the time, MacArthur must have been a real object of admiration among the women, the image of the most "masculine" sort of man.

I have already mentioned how useful the letters to MacArthur were as sources of information for the Occupation army, but let me say something about one letter in particular that was crucial in the case of the search for Ba Maw. The story goes back to before the war, but in August 1943, in the midst of the Pacific War, Burma, which was serving as one wing of the "Greater East Asian Co-Prosperity Sphere," became "independent," as did the Philippines in October of the same year. At the time the chairman of the government of Burma was Ba Maw. With Japan's defeat, Ba Maw took refuge in Japan. From the point of view of Burma's suzerain state, Britain, Ba Maw was the ringleader of those in Burma who cooperated with the Japanese, and he had to be punished. Thus he was in hiding and waiting for the clamor to subside in a Buddhist temple in the village of Ishiuchi in Minami-Uonuma county in Niigata Prefecture, on the Japan Sea coast of Japan. Ishiuchi is known now for its ski resort, but in early postwar Japan, when people were hardly in a position to enjoy skiing, it was nothing more than a remote mountain village with a lot of snow.

One day, around the end of 1945, a letter arrived for General MacArthur from this village in Niigata Prefecture. The letter said:

"There is a strange monk living in our village who clearly does not appear to be Japanese. He stays in the temple all day long and never goes outside, not even briefly. To judge from his appearance and actions, I suspect that he is a war criminal who is living here in hiding. Please be kind enough to look into this." To my recollection, this was the content of the letter as we translated it. I remember that the word "war criminal" was being used everywhere in those days. We immediately translated this letter into English and sent it to MacArthur's headquarters, and the headquarters immediately sent it on to CIC (Counter Intelligence Corps).

When CIC received the letter, they ordered one of their

members, Lieutenant Frank Alweis, to go to the village in Niigata and find out who this monk was. Frank was an old acquaintance of mine who had been in the same class with me at the Japanese language school, so he came and paid me a visit before he left on his investigation trip. He said, "Do you know anything else about this matter? If you do, tell me." Of course there was no way I could know anything more than what I had translated in the letter. "I have to go and investigate this. Actually, that is a terribly remote place with lots of snow, isn't it? And I have to go all on my own." Alweis left my office, carrying the famous C-rations, with a look of anxiety on his face that could not be concealed.

What I heard several days later, after he returned to Tokyo, was, in his own words, "First, I went to find the person who wrote the letter. 'I am so and so and such and such a person,' I said. 'I have come here on General MacArthur's behalf in connection with the matter you raised in the letter you sent to the General.'

"After introducing myself in this manner, the man offered to take me to the temple where the mysterious monk was staying. Since I had no idea what might happen, I had taken a pistol with me when I left Tokyo. As I approached the temple I held tightly to my pistol so that I would be ready for anything that happened.

"It turned out to be a really tiny temple, and when we got there the guy said, 'You go into the temple by yourself. I hereby take my leave.'

"I had no choice, so I steeled myself and entered the temple. And just like the letter had said, inside the room a lone monk was just sitting there. In Japanese he asked me, 'Who are you, sir? My name is Ba Maw. I am the Prime Minister of Burma.'

"I answered in English, 'So you are Mr. Ba Maw! I came to

meet you.' He stood up as though he had been waiting wearily for this time to come, put his things into a little bag, and began to prepare to leave the temple.

"So I brought Ba Maw back with me to Tokyo by train from snowy Niigata Prefecture."

What became of Ba Maw after this goes beyond my topic at hand, so I do not want to go into it. But I would just like to add that after he arrived in Tokyo, he was not judged as a war criminal but allowed to return to Burma as a free man. I think that Ba Maw was probably looking for a way to get out of the snowy mountain temple in Niigata and thus "hoping" to be discovered by the Allied forces, thinking that the time was just about ripe for him to return to his country. The image I got from Frank's story was that Ba Maw was clearly waiting anxiously for Frank's visit.

My Views of General MacArthur

I HAVE BEEN WRITING about the letters written by Japanese people to General MacArthur, but just what sort of person was MacArthur, to attract such letters?

There have been quite a few detailed books published on MacArthur in both Japan and the U.S. The best is probably *The Age of MacArthur*, by Clayton James, in three volumes. Then there are works by historians such as Carol Petillo and Justin Williams, political scientists like Theodore MacNelly, and Japanese scholars like Sodei Rinjiro and Hata Ikuhiko, and Takemae Eiji. Actually, as a person living in Japan as an officer, working in GHQ SCAP, for me too he was my big boss, so I have my own personal views about him that I will outline here.

First I would like to consider just why it is that it was MacArthur, and not someone else, who landed in Japan as the Supreme Commander of the Allied Powers. For, as one of his subordinates, this is closely connected to the reasons why I myself landed in Japan. The reason, needless to say, is that, in effect, it was he who directed the entire course of the Pacific War.

The war began with a miserable defeat. Even though before the Pacific War broke out MacArthur boasted that he would defend the Philippines from any attack from the Japanese, after the war began, his forces suffered painful defeats in Bataan and Corregidor. While in actuality he left most of his subordinates in the Philippines under the leadership of General Jonathan Wainwright, MacArthur himself was compelled to escape with his family by submarine to Australia by way of Mindanao in the southern Philippines. This was an event that symbolized the defeat and retreat of America at the beginning of the war, and his famous statement, "I shall return" became the slogan of that generation.

Then, from 1942, came the American counterattack beginning with a step-by-step progress from one island to the next in the Southwest Pacific. The joint U.S.-Australian army that MacArthur led advanced upward from New Guinea to the Philippines to Okinawa, driving the Japanese army more and more into a corner as they progressed.

In any case, the Japanese surrender mission headed for MacArthur's headquarters in the Philippines, and it was MacArthur himself who received them and signed the surrender documents aboard the *U.S.S. Missouri* on behalf of the Allied forces.

If one looks back over the entire course of the Pacific War from beginning to end, perhaps it seems that this was an extremely natural way for things to unfold. For even President Truman could not have appointed another person in MacArthur's place as the Supreme Commander of the Occupation forces in Japan. Truly, in the General Headquarters there was not one other person who would have been appropriate to serve as the Supreme Commander of Allied Forces, and MacArthur maintained his supreme position in GHQ right through until he was dismissed by President Truman in 1951.

Then, just what were the characteristics of MacArthur's policies in his position as de facto ruler of Japan during the Occupation? A lot of things have been said about MacArthur. He has been called the "blue-eyed Shogun," the "naked king," and so on. However, when I try to understand him, I think that what is most worthy of attention is his role as a "colonial ruler." Why? Because, as becomes clear if one looks at his career, his study and experience while living in America's colony, the Philippines, came to be strongly projected onto his rule of Japan.

MacArthur's connection with the Philippines was long and deep, extending to his father's as well as his own generation. At the time of the Spanish-American War, his father, General Arthur MacArthur, served as director of strategy and brigade commander in the American Army in the Philippines landing force. On the strength of his merit in that role, he became an official in the military government of the Philippines, and his third son, Douglas, was also assigned to the Philippines as his first overseas posting after graduating from Army Officers School in 1903. Then, after he resigned his position as Chief of the General Staff in 1935, the post that Douglas MacArthur sought was again the role of army commander in the Philippine Commonwealth. Thenceforth, for six years he poured all his energy into tightening the Philippine defenses in preparation for a Japanese invasion. It is not necessary to repeat what the result of all this was. At the same time as the Pacific War broke out in December 1941, the Japanese army boldly undertook a landing operation in the Philippines with an overwhelming force. The U.S.-Philippine forces were easily broken and forced to retreat, and MacArthur and his family escaped from the fortress at Corregidor Island, the gateway to Manila, and headed for Australia.

If we keep this whole background in mind, it will not seem strange that, fulfilling his promise that "I shall return," he first reclaimed the Philippines, and then, after landing in Japan as Supreme Commander of Allied Forces, he implemented policies that were deeply colored by his experience in the Philippines. From the start he never had a particularly deep knowledge of or interest in Japanese culture, society, and history. Accordingly, the image of ruling Japan that he had in his mind at the time of the Occupation was the same as the one that he had become deeply accustomed to in his many years in the Philippines.

When he landed in Japan as supreme commander, the Daiichi Seimei Building he chose as the location of his headquarters, the building he chose for his residence with his family, and the building used for the American embassy all had white walls. These buildings bore a close resemblance to the white Malacanan Palace where the American Philippine Governor General lived and the white Manila Hotel where MacArthur lived with his family as commander of the Philippine army. Together with the fact that he occupied the highest floor in both the Daiichi Seimei Building and the Manila Hotel, it is clear that his transfer to Japan carried with it many similarities to his work in the Philippines.

In addition, the coolness and inapproachability of his manner, his grandiloquence, his arrogance, and so on, were much more like the style of a colonial viceroy than an emperor. In this point, one could probably say he bore a close resemblance to Lord Mountbatten, Viceroy of India, or Van Mook, Governor General of the Dutch East Indies. In this new American colonial

"Viceroy," the Japanese, as well, could see a resemblance to their own colonial viceroys of Taiwan and Korea, the governor-general of the Kwantung Japanese leasehold in the Liaotung Peninsula, or the Chief of the Department of the South Seas, and in this image they respected him.

Accordingly, I think that MacArthur's conception that American-style democracy must be planted in Japan arose very naturally as an extension of his experience in the Philippines. In the case of the Philippines, under the name of the "deeply compassionate" American colonial authority, American-style democracy and an American-style constitution were forcefully implemented, in the belief that the country could be granted independence only after the "not-yet-civilized" Filipino masses had been awakened. Thus, on the basis of the Tydings-MacDuffie Act of 1934, a constitution was enacted in 1935. I believe that this process was very strongly imprinted on MacArthur's mind during the Occupation of Japan. Therefore, he landed in Japan with a "mission" of democratizing the Japanese people, and policies like the enactment of a new constitution were, in that sense, already decided in his mind.

It seems that the Japanese government did not understand this line of connection very well, or that they were incapable of understanding it, and MacArthur became very impatient with the way the directives of SCAP were met constantly with delaying tactics on the part of the Japanese. In the matter of the constitution as well, the Japanese government attempted simply to make some partial revisions to the Meiji Constitution, but from the point of view of the American side, with its proud belief that America represented the highest development of democracy, Japan possessed no constitution that was worthy of being revised. As a matter of fact, in the Philippines, under American rule, right in the midst of an anti-American uprising that broke out in 1899, the Malolos Constitution was drafted, but after the Occupation the Americans paid no attention to this native constitution, and the Meiji Constitution was no different. Political leadership based on the ideal of American-style democracy was the basis of American colonialism, and it was the basic principle of American rule in countries that are or were American colonies—the Philippines, Puerto Rico, Guam, American Samoa, Micronesia. It goes without saying that Japan was no exception. It is just that, in the case of Japan, the prewar influence of America was relatively light, so that the encounter with American-style democracy probably had greater shock power than was expected. In addition, I think that because the Japanese attack on Pearl Harbor was a flagrant act against democracy, the U.S. ended up imposing its own idea of democracy on Japan even more forcefully. In this situation, the problem of the Japanese constitution was of the greatest importance.

In addition to MacArthur's belief that American-style democracy and an American-style constitution must be implanted in Japan, he also believed in the necessity of American-style religious preaching. This was because if Japan were a Christian country, he thought, something like Pearl Harbor would never have occurred. So he tried hard to bring Christianity into Japan. Actually, the spiritual emptiness that the Japanese felt because of the defeat and the destruction of their cities was extreme, and because of that it was an easy thing to spread Christianity among them. To take advantage of this unprecedented opportunity, MacArthur imposed the manifestly contradictory policy of, on the one hand, guaranteeing freedom of religion, and, on the other hand, promoting Christian proselytization. He did everything possible to facilitate the evangelical activities of American missionaries and religious leaders, assisted in the foundation of International Christian University, and so forth. He assumed that if Japan became a Christian country, the Occupation would go very smoothly.

Yet in spite of all of these efforts on his part, the proportion of Christians in Japan has declined in comparison to what it was before the war. So it is obvious that his policy did not produce the results that he intended. Nevertheless, through seeing how important Christianity was to MacArthur in the process of "civilizing" Japan, the Japanese could get a glimpse into just how great a role this religion has played in the history and spread of Western civilization.

To continue further in this direction, I think that the agricultural land reform program was intimately connected to MacArthur's Christian-style administration. This is because I think that it was a Biblical-style belief that the poverty-stricken peasants must be saved from their "slave-like condition under the feudal system" that moved MacArthur to turn his attention to land reform. It is true that, when he traveled to India with his parents in the autumn of 1905 at the invitation of an Englishman, he said that he was deeply impressed by the orderly and efficient nature of England's "superb colonial rule." However, he was even more familiar with the democratic atmosphere of American society and the realities of America's colonial rule in the Philippines. For that reason, seeing himself as a devout Christian, he firmly believed that saving the poverty-stricken peasants of Asia was a particular duty of the colonial rulers.

Thus he felt a kind of responsibility for the peasants of Japan, and he undoubtedly judged that it was essential that their lives be improved. This is why he ventured to compare the Japanese land reforms to the liberation of the serfs by Alexander II of Russia and the liberation of the slaves in America by Lincoln. This way of looking at the matter, in a sense, can perhaps be said to have been a bit naïve and excessively "historical." Nevertheless, I think that one cannot deny the role of MacArthur's faith in Christianity in inspiring this land reform policy.

If we consider the matter from this perspective, I think that MacArthur emerges as a highly charismatic, religious, patriotic, romantic individual with a strong desire to completely reform the Japanese people.

If we look closely at the road that he walked, we cannot help but think that he was a nineteenth-century individual who tried to apply that century's simple and Arcadian principles in the complex world of international politics in the twentieth century. And the fact that he succeeded in the ruling of Japan was, I think, due to his extraordinary and dignified character. For his view of the world, and the posture that that view gave rise to, was, on the one hand, capable of putting powerful pressure on his own country while he was pushing through the reforms in Japan, and on the other hand, played an important role in propelling the Japanese, with their submissiveness to authority, to obey his decrees.

Accordingly, the fact that postwar Japan played an important role in the process of America's policy decisions and in the working out of the Japan-U.S. alliance, I believe, owed a great deal to the influence of MacArthur's personality. Why? Because his personality exerted great influence in asserting the principle of "Japan first," in opposition to public opinion makers and policymakers in America who favored the contrary principles of "Europe first," "China first," or "India first."

11

My View of the Constitution

THE TOPIC OF THE Japanese Constitution is something that must be discussed by a historian of Japan who lived there as an officer in the Occupation army during the period that the problem was being debated, from 1945 to 1946. I touched very briefly on the constitution problem in my chapter discussing MacArthur, but here I would like to continue the discussion by focusing on three topics that have always been of great concern to me.

The first topic concerns what kind of views and ideas the American side held at the time of revision of the constitution. The second is the task of retracing the entire process of the revision of the constitution from the time of Japan's surrender to the time of the enactment of the new constitution. The third topic involves examining some provisions and problem points in the new constitution in relation to the American Constitution.

Regarding the first topic, I think that it is necessary to look first at the role played by the American conception of constitutionalism in the democratization of Japan, which included the rewriting of the constitution. We should not forget that in the U.S. at that time the constitution was the spiritual, religious, and moral symbol of the American people. For a country that had been founded only 150 years earlier and for which no other symbol could be found but the constitution, perhaps this was something perfectly natural. Moreover, there was a sense of mission deeply rooted among the American people that respect for this constitution should not be limited to the American people, but should be spread widely among the people of "not-yet-civilized" alien cultures. Therefore, post-surrender Japan became another of the new territories which the Americans believed should be brought under the influence of the American constitution.

In expectation of an American victory in the war against Japan, as early as April 1942 the American leaders began considering what policy should be adopted toward Japan after the war. The main principles were to reconstruct the Japanese political system along American lines and to build a new Japan that would be incapable of surprise attacks like that represented by Pearl Harbor. For that reason, it was very important to replace the "origin of all evils"—as the Meiji Constitution was viewed—with a new American-style constitution.

In addition, the person who landed in Japan as the Supreme Commander of Allied Forces was none other than Douglas MacArthur. His character and experience and his basic ideas regarding the constitution have already been discussed in the previous chapter. He had a deep-rooted belief that was a kind of *idée fixe* regarding the necessity of enacting a new constitution in Japan, and he firmly believed that the Meiji Constitution served to rationalize the actions of the Japanese militarists in attacking Pearl Harbor and invading the Philippines. Thus, under his aegis, an American-style constitution came to be forcefully introduced to Japan.

Another reason MacArthur was impatient to put an American-style constitution into effect was that the enmity between the U.S. and the Soviet Union was deepening right about that time. After the death of President Roosevelt, there came the occupation of Germany, the entry of the Soviet Union into the war against Japan, the dropping of the atomic bombs, and the Japanese surrender, a course of events through which the Soviet Union tried to gain a greater and greater voice in the Occupation policy toward Japan. For the U.S., it was necessary to find out in advance the reform directives of the Far Eastern Commission in Washington, of which the USSR was a member, and to initiate a large number of reforms to assure that they could stay one step ahead of Stalin. And it was necessary that these reforms be American-style and not Soviet-style reforms.

And finally, to add one more condition, I think that the American side—especially the Japan specialists in the U.S.—had an extremely high estimation of the significance of Japan's experience of "Taishō democracy" from 1912 to 1926. The factor that acted as an obstruction to the development of Japanese democracy in this "Taishō democracy" period, they thought, was precisely the Meiji Constitution promulgated in 1889, so that for the promoters of reform in both Washington and Tokyo, if the Meiji Constitution was abolished and a new constitution enacted, one could expect an upsurge of democracy many times more intensive than that of the Taishō period.

This sums up the various dimensions of the attitude of the American side at the time of the enactment of the new constitution. Now I would like to look at the matter from a chronological point of view and follow the actual course of the constitutional revision from the time of Japan's surrender to the final formulation of the constitution.

The process began when, on October 4, 1945, MacArthur suggested the revision of the constitution and the expansion of the right of political participation to the Minister of State, Konoe Fumimaro. Konoe obtained the assistance of Professor Sasaki Sōichi of Kyoto Imperial University and commenced work on constitutional revision. However, just at that time the problem surfaced of Konoe's designation as a war criminal, and MacArthur declared that Konoe's work on constitution revision had no connection with him. Accordingly, Konoe's work was nipped in the bud. Having been designated a war criminal, Konoe committed suicide on December 16 by taking poison.

Also, on October 9, MacArthur directed the Shidehara Kijurō cabinet, successor to the Higashikuni cabinet, to take up the matter of revising the Meiji Constitution as its most important task. In addition, he passed the cabinet a list of points relating to the democratization of society and the economy as a whole, and pressed them to work quickly for their implementation. Shidehara appointed former Tokyo Imperial University professor, Matsumoto Jōji, as Minister of State, organized a committee for the investigation of the constitutional problem with Matsumoto as head, and had them set to work immediately on the concrete details of the work.

On January 7, 1946, a document called SWNCC 228, "Reform of the Japanese Ruling System," drafted by the Coordinating Committee of the Department of State, the War Department, and the Department of the Navy, arrived on MacArthur's desk through the Integrated Staff Office. Even MacArthur, who up to that time had shunned interference by the State Department in the Japanese Occupation administration, believed firmly, on the basis of this directive, that Washington was hoping very strongly for constitutional reform, and, accordingly, he promoted the concrete implementation of the reform.

On February 1, 1946, the Matsumoto draft constitution was scooped by the *Mainichi Shimbun*, and at the same time, in conjunction with other research reports, a constitution problem consultation report was submitted to GHQ-SCAP. The Matsumoto draft was nothing more than a partial revision of the Meiji Constitution, so it could hardly satisfy the desire of GHQ for a drastic reform.

Thereupon GHQ, under the direction of General Courtney Whitney, head of the Government Section of SCAP, took up the pen themselves and began writing a draft constitution for the Japanese nation following the line of the SWNCC 228. I understand that Whitney's order was to produce a draft "quickly and in strict secrecy," which were necessary conditions to avoid alarming the Japanese and to prevent the Japanese from interfering in the GHQ's constitution draft. There were three core points in MacArthur's directive to Whitney: (1) the retention of the Emperor system as a symbol only; (2) the renunciation of war; (3) a clean sweeping away of the vestiges of feudalism, including the abolition of the aristocratic system and the nationalization of imperial family property.

In this way, the work of drafting the constitution was continued within the Government Section divided into nine sections of responsibility. In this work, General Whitney was at the helm, and he was assisted by Colonel Charles Kades of the army and Commander Hersey of the navy. Moreover, in connection with the article regarding the equal rights for women, the lead was taken by Ms. Beate Sirota Gordon.

None of the participants had ever written a constitution before, so it was a tremendous task. Since I was in Japan as an officer in the Occupation army and had a friend who was involved in the drafting process, I can report that the most useful thing in the drafting process was a book in English found in the library of the Law Faculty of the Imperial University of Tokyo called *Constitutions of the World*. The library of Tokyo University had not been burned in the air raids, and it had a great collection of books, but what pleased the responsible officials in the Occupation forces more than anything was this book, which contained the constitutions of virtually every country arranged in alphabetical order. The book was consulted in considering the wording of every article of the new Japanese constitution.

The resulting GHQ draft constitution was shown to the Japanese government representatives on February 13, 1946. At 10:00 A.M. on that day, a meeting was held which included General Whitney, Colonel Kades, and others on the American side, and Yoshida Shigeru, Minister of Foreign Affairs, and Matsumoto Jōji, Minister of State, on the Japanese side. The draft they were shown, with its provision for the symbolic Emperor system, the renunciation of war, and so on, was precisely the same as the Japanese constitution which is still in effect. One can imagine how much this draft surprised Yoshida and Matsumoto, who had been trying to get by with a moderate revision of the Meiji Constitution.

Whitney, Kades, Yoshida and Matsumoto appeared on NHK in about 1978 on a program called "Two Hours in the Sun Room: the Shock of the GHQ Constitution Draft." This was later compiled by NHK into a book called "Japan's Postwar" (*Nihon no sengo*). Since the details of the meeting are thus well known, and also covered well in English-language books, I will refrain from discussing them in detail here. I will simply note that Matsumoto's comments about the draft were that it was "far too radical," that it "does not fit with the conditions of our country," and that "it casts a dark cloud over the future of Japan." Yoshida's comments were equally severe. It was not only "revolutionary," he said, but "incoherent and absurd." Moreover, ironically, when Yoshida later attacked Shidehara and took over as prime minister, he had no choice but to do everything in his power to push through the approval of this draft in the Diet. On November 3, 1946, the Constitution of Japan was promulgated, and it took effect on May 3 of the following year.

I have traced the historical process of the revision of the constitution, but to grasp its essence, I think it is necessary to give some attention to the following three points. One is the fact that even though Japan had been the object of severe condemnation during the Second World War, this American-style constitution became the nation's trump card when she re-emerged on the international stage. The second is the fact that, during the Cold War, the only force that was effective against Marxism and international Communism led by the Soviet Union was American-style bourgeois constitutionalism, and that the existence of this counterforce was essential. The third is the fact that, in the light of the above two conditions, there was insufficient time—that is to say, SCAP was unable to wait any longer for the Japanese, who were not aware of the seriousness of the international situation, to come up with a constitution draft, so they took the job into their own hands.

Accordingly, it goes without saying that the influence of the U.S. on the postwar Japanese constitution is extremely deep. The fact that the idea of "basic human rights" appears again and again throughout the constitution is one example. If this was a result of Japan's acceptance of the Potsdam Declaration, which promised to "build a government that will seek peace on the basis of the free will of the Japanese people," then it can be said to have been extremely natural.

At any rate, although the constitution of Japan was formulated under very strong American influence, SCAP claimed unyieldingly that this constitution was made by the Japanese people themselves, and the Occupation censors strictly forbade the Japanese newspapers from looking into this matter. On the one hand, MacArthur called for discussion of the new constitution on the part of the Japanese people, but on the other hand he used great skill to control this discussion and manipulate public opinion in the direction of support for the new constitution. The man who grasped the thinking of SCAP and took care of the matter skillfully in the Diet was none other than Yoshida Shigeru. In that sense, he acted as a good "soldier" under General MacArthur.

I have discussed in a very general way the historical process of the reform of the constitution, and next I would like to look at the characteristics of certain articles of the constitution in comparison with the American Constitution. First, the most prominent characteristic of the new constitution was the exaltation of the principle of the sovereignty of the people over the principle that sovereignty rested with the Emperor. As a result, as stipulated in "Chapter One: The Emperor," the Emperor became a "symbol" in the same way as Queen Elizabeth is in Britain. The advocacy of popular sovereignty in place of Imperial sovereignty is the basic line that runs through all the articles of the constitution, and the thoroughness with which this principle is put forward greatly exceeds that of the U.S. Constitution. The fact that over one-third of the one hundred thirty-three articles of the constitution extol the principle of basic human rights is a case in point.

This was not, I think, without reason. In the Second World War, the idea of basic human rights was manifestly lacking within the Axis powers, particularly in Germany, and an emphasis on human rights was necessary to assure that Japan would not again take the side of the totalitarian states. That is to say, the emphasis on basic human rights in the Japanese constitution incorporated the bitter experience that led up to the Second World War and a great deal of reflection on that experience.

Next, let us consider "Chapter Three: The Rights and Duties of Citizens." One notices that all kinds of rights and duties are stipulated therein. First, Article 15 stipulates that "It is an inherent right of the people to select civil service officials and dismiss them in the case of wrongdoing" ("an inherent right of the people" appears to be a Japanese expression). Then the constitution goes on to guarantee ordinary elections using secret ballots, the right of petition, the responsibility of the state and public bodies to give compensation in the cases of loss, freedom from slave-like restraint and forced labor, freedom of thought and conscience, freedom of religion, the prohibition of religious activities on the part of the state, freedom of assembly, association, and expression, the confidentiality of communications, and so on.

The writers of the draft constitution believed that these freedoms had not existed, that Japan had been able to embark on the road to unrestrained foreign invasion, and that without these freedoms Japan would not be able to move toward becoming a democratic and peaceful country after the war.

Accordingly, there are even some Japanese scholars who refer to the GHQ staff who drafted the constitution as "red." While this is an extreme view, it is a fact that most of the young, core staff members were from the generation that had received its intellectual training in the age of the New Deal, with its leftist leanings, and it is an undisputed fact that they attempted to bring New Deal principles into the Japanese Constitution. However, no matter how these young, core staff members may have thought, if their ideas did not get the OK from MacArthur and Whitney, these provisions would not have gotten incorporated into the constitution draft. In that sense, it was the ideas of these two men that were decisive.

The fact that these two, who had conservative ideas, did not pick quarrels with the more progressive young staff in the course of the drafting of the constitution is worth noting, but if one thinks about it, there was really nothing particularly strange about it. This is because, generally speaking, it is misplaced to argue about whether the process of the enactment of the constitution was conservative or progressive. Rather, the problem should be considered on the level of the formation of "permanent peace" and "a democratic Japan" at the hands of Americans whose handiwork should be respected.

There are many other points that could be discussed in comparison with the American Constitution, but since I have no space to examine each article one by one I will conclude my discussion of the constitution by touching upon the problem of Article 9, which renounces the use of war and denies Japan the right to maintain military forces or engage in military actions.

As is well known, there is a great deal of controversy over just who incorporated this article into the constitution. The idea of having the constitution renounce the use of war was first put forward by Kades, a deputy of General Whitney. It is said that when the Kellogg-Briand Pact was concluded in Paris in 1928, Kades was a tireless promoter of this "no-war treaty," and Article 9 in the Japanese constitution is actually taken from this Kellogg-Briand Pact. In any case, if MacArthur had not agreed with Kades's advocacy of this principle, no matter how much Kades had pushed for it, it would have been virtually impossible for it to be included in the constitution. Thus, it is clear that the conception of renunciation of war was advocated strongly by

MacArthur as well. It seems that MacArthur thought it desirable to place Japan in a state of disarmament and allow it only the least possible amount of military power, which was to be kept strictly under the control of civilian officials. At any rate, Article 9 was intended to sweep away Japan's militaristic past and, following the precedent of the Kellogg-Briand Pact, was incorporated into the constitution in the hope that militarism would never be reborn.

Finally, there is the fact that, in the case of the U.S., the president is the supreme commander of the military, but in the case of Japan, according to Article 9, there is no equivalent provision. Later, of course, the Self-Defense Force was established, but it should be noted that its civilian control is achieved by custom.

Be that as it may, constitutions are in an ultimate sense, nothing more than pieces of paper, and what makes them effective are the untiring efforts of the citizens of the country. For that reason, I would like to emphasize that, in spite of the strong foreign influence on the drafting of the constitution, it was designed for the Japanese people, and that in the sixty-odd years since its implementation, it has become Japanized to the extent that its American origin has almost disappeared from sight.

12

The Movements of Reform —
The Dynamic and the Static

ALLOW ME TO CHANGE the mood a bit by moving away from the rather serious topics of MacArthur and the constitution to talk about my experiences of interesting things like the movement for reform, the demonstrations, and the movement advocating the romanization of Japanese.

First, the demonstrations. As an Occupation officer in Japan from the autumn of 1945 to the autumn of 1946, I really got to see all kinds of demonstrations. One reason was that the NYK Building, my office, was close to Tokyo Station, located in the Marunouchi district, and facing the Imperial Palace. Accordingly, when I passed by my window, I was often met with the sight of demonstrators marching through the streets, and I heard their choruses of shouts and yells. Carrying flags, wearing headbands, and shouting slogans in loud voices, they snaked around the buildings repeatedly in a zigzag fashion.

My first thoughts when I saw them, to speak frankly, were

that this was childish behavior like that of innocent children who give no thought to the trouble they are causing other people. I had never seen such demonstrations in America. I felt strongly that they were more like crowds of mischievous boys making a ruckus than demonstrations.

"It seems," I thought, "that the Japanese don't understand much about what democracy is." In a word, that was my impression of the demonstrations. I will withhold judgment as to whether my impressions were correct or not, but it is undeniable that that is the impression I had at the time.

If the demonstrators had understood American-style democracy, would they have marched in that way, shouting and yelling as they went, without regard to the trouble they were causing other people? I think probably not. Instead, they would probably have formed a political party and directed their energies to building up the party so that it could become the majority party through elections.

At any rate, the American Occupation authorities at the time did not think this sort of demonstration was a good thing, but that does not mean that they prohibited or suppressed them. Of course, it would have been a different thing if people had been killed or injured or some other serious consequences had ensued. But as long as it did not come to that, the Occupation authorities were tolerant of this type of activity. At least this tolerance prevailed while I was in Japan from 1945 to 1946. By the time of the general strike that was called on February 1st, 1947, the Occupation side also changed *their* policy and began to take an attitude of resistance.

The tolerance of the Allied forces toward the demonstrations presented a marked contrast to the policy of the Japanese government before the war, which was one of harsh repression. The populace, who had groaned under the weight of government repression and a police force known for their cruel suppression of popular protest, were liberated for the first time by the defeat, and became free to engage in collective action. Breathing deeply the unaccustomed air of freedom, people spread their wings, and in their longing to relieve their accumulated stress, reacted to the wretched circumstances of life at the time, and their anxiety and resentment about unemployment, in particular, exploded in these great demonstrations: "During the long years of war in China and of the Pacific War, we have been repressed and forced to endure great austerity. Now whatever we do we are free." It was as if a child who had long been confined to his house all day long was suddenly told by his mother, "It's OK. Go outside and play!" Given permission to go out, with great joy the child leaps outside and seeks every way possible to give vent to his bottled-up energy, jumping and running around excitedly and getting into all kinds of mischief.

If the demonstration movements were the "dynamic" side of the condition of society, then perhaps the movement for the use of Roman letters was the "static" side. It was not showy or loud, but I think it was also a large-scale problem. Especially in the period when I was an Occupation officer, between 1945 and 1946, the movement to abandon the use of Chinese characters and use Roman letters to write Japanese was thriving. Whether as a reflection of this movement or as something that preceded the movement, within the CIE (Civil Information and Education Section)—the body within GHQ responsible for the problem of education—there was quite a vehement argument over whether Roman letters or Chinese characters should be used. A close friend of mine was a member of the CIE, so I was able to hear about the situation in some detail. And I know the controversy was not confined to the CIE but was also attracting great attention within the higher levels of the GHQ.

The view of those in the GHQ who were pushing for the use of Roman letters was as follows:

Kanji take a lot of time to learn, which would result in a large-scale sacrifice of time that should be devoted to education in democracy. That is to say, because of the large amount of time taken in learning *kanji*, their use would result in the sacrifice of time needed to cultivate the way of thinking on the part of the individual essential to education in a democracy and time needed for education in American-style individualism.

For the advocates of retaining *kanji*, their views were as follows:

The romanization of Japanese is technologically impossible, because as a purely phonetic script it provides no effective way to represent a language in which there are a large number of words with the same pronunciation but completely different meanings.

Being an American, I was not opposed to the idea of romanization, and I was not convinced by the arguments of the advocates of retaining the use of *kanji*. I thought that the problem of deciphering different words written with the same phonetic characters would be solved easily by judgment based on context. This was definitely not an unfounded view. When I was being trained as a military intelligence officer at Fort Snelling I dealt with a large number of military telegraph messages written in Roman letters, and there was not even one case where the meaning was unclear just because of the message being written in romaji. If one judged from the context it was always easy to infer the meaning. Moreover, before the war Turkish and Vietnamese were successfully romanized. I saw no reason why this wouldn't be possible for Japanese.

Let me give an illustration of how strong the romanization movement was from the end of 1945 through 1946 by reference to the children's picture books that I collected at the time. When I had breaks from my work, I much enjoyed making the rounds of the local bookstores. On one such occasion, which I think was in the early summer of 1946, I discovered some children's books written in romaji. For instance, on the side of a book called *The Children and the Dog*, the word for "dog" (*inu*) was written in romaji and the English word for "dog" was added as well. I think that there were quite a few such picture books on the market at this time. One representative example was, I think, the magazine *Kokumin ichinensei*, published by Shogakukan. As was clear if one looked at the cover, the original title of the magazine had been *Shōgaku ichinensei* (Elementary School, First Year); the name had been changed when the elementary schools were renamed "citizens' schools" (*kokumin gakkō*) during the war. This name, written in katakana, was still in use in this period after the war, and below it "KOKUMIN ICHINENSEI" was written prominently in romaji. From this one can get an idea of the height of the wave of romanization at this time in Japan. However, this romanization movement later came to an end without producing any fruits. Evidently the adoption of the limited list of 1850 *kanji* for daily use (*Tōyō Kanji*) in November, 1946, was the product of a compromise between the advocates of romanization or the exclusive use of kana on the one hand and the opponents of the abandonment of *kanji* on the other. Official simplified forms of writing many of the more complex *kanji* were not promulgated until 1949, but this move can also be regarded as a later expression of the compromise between the two positions in the controversy.

Grant Goodman in uniform.

Grant Goodman wearing a
kimono over his military
uniform (1945).

ABOVE: Army Intensive Japanese Language School Faculty in their office, Angell Hall, University of Michigan (1943). BELOW: Army Intensive Japanese Language School. Inspection in formation, West Quadrangle, University of Michigan (1943).

ABOVE: Army Intensive Japanese Language School. Faculty, Angell Hall, University of Michigan (1943). BELOW: Colonel Kai Rasmussen addressing students of the Army Intensive Japanese Language School, Rackham Hall, University of Michigan (1943).

Army Intensive Japanese Language School students at a rehearsal of an original musical called "Nips in the Bud." Grant Goodman is in the second row, third from the left (Lydia Mendelssohn Theater, University of Michigan, 1944).

Japanese language class under the trees outside Angell Hall, University of Michigan. Grant Goodman is sitting to the immediate right of the instructor (1943).

Fort McClellan, Alabama. Grant Goodman is third from the right in line (1944).

Fort McClellan, Alabama. Grant Goodman is front center (1944).

Ernie Pyle Theater, Tokyo.
BELOW: Side view of NYK Building with Imperial Palace moat.

Nijūbashi, the bridge over the Imperial Palace moat, Tokyo.

Kokumin Ichinensei
(September 1946)

Right: Ueno Station
(1945).

Below: Entrance pass
to International
Military Tribunal,
Far East

INTERNATIONAL MILITARY TRIBUNAL,
FAR EAST

SPECTATORS PASS

GOOD FOR ONE TRIAL SESSION
WAR MINISTRY BUILDING

協議許可證

AM

James T Larson, 1st Lt.
ATTENDANCE CONTROL OFFICER

VALID ON DATE SHOWN   ISSUING AGENCY

NOTE:

1. No smoking in court at any time.
2. Use of cameras in court room is prohibited.
3. Spectators leaving at any recess forfeit right to retire to court room.
4. Morning Session spectators must be seated not later than 0915.
   Afternoon Session spectators must be seated not later than 1315.
5. Pass will be surrendered to Military Police on request.

INTERNATIONAL MILITARY TRIBUNAL, FAR EAST
COURT ROOM SEATING DIAGRAM
(READING FROM STAGE TO BALCONY)

JUDGES	DEFENDANTS	
	FRONT ROW	BACK ROW
JARANILLA (PHILIPPINE)	1. DOIHARA	1. HASHIMOTO
NORTHCROFT (NEW ZEALAND)	2. HATA	2. KOISO
	3. HIROTA	3. NAGANO
BERNARD (FRANCE)	4. MINAMI	4. OSHIMA
ZARYANOV (U. S. S. R.)		5. MATSUI
MEI (CHINA)	1. TOJO	
WEBB (AUSTRALIA)	2. OKA	1. HIRANUMA
	3. UMEZU	2. TOGO
CRAMER (U. S. A.)	4. ARAKI	3. SHIGEMITSU
PATRICK (GREAT BRITAIN)	5. MUTO	
McDOUGALL (CANADA)	1. HOSHINO	1. SATO
	2. KAYA	2. SHIMADA
ROLING (NETHERLANDS)	3. KIDO	3. SHIRATORI
PAL (INDIA)	4. KIMURA	4. SUZUKI
		5. ITAGAKI

NOTE:

1. No smoking in court at any time.

2. Use of cameras in courtroom is prohibited except by accredited photographers.

3. Spectators leaving at any recess forfeit right to return to courtroom for that session.

4. A. M. spectators must be seated not later than 0915. P. M. spectators must be seated not later than 1315.

5. Pass will be surrendered to Military Police on request.

6. There is one set of headphones provided for each spectator. Use only the headphone you will find at your seat. Do not tamper with sound equipment.

7. When Judges enter courtroom stand and remain silent.

8. After the departure of the Judges all persons are required to be seated until defendants leave the courtroom.

13

The Appearance of Emperor Kumazawa

SINCE IT WAS during the period I was working in the department for translating letters to MacArthur, it must have been around the end of 1945 or somewhat before that. One day while I was working in my office in the NYK building, there was a great commotion outside. The translation department was always extremely quiet, but on this day only, there was a great hubbub of voices, and with so many people rushing between the desks to get to the windows, it was impossible to settle down.

What on earth was going on? I made my way to the place where all the commotion was. A gentleman with a noble countenance accompanied by several Japanese companions was trying to enter the building, and the group was having an animated argument with the MPs who were guarding the entrance.

One of the colleagues standing on the outside of the site of the commotion asked me, "Lieutenant Goodman, what the heck is going on? Who is this guy and what does he want to say?"

"I don't know myself," I answered. But this was hardly something that I could just ignore and get back to my work. So I asked the gentleman in Japanese, "Who are you, sir, and what is it that brings you here?"

"I am Emperor Kumazawa."

Emperor Kumazawa?

At first I thought that this fellow must be out of his mind or something. However, to judge from his countenance and his attitude, this did not seem to be the case. Was it a joke? If it was a joke, just what sort of a joke could it be?

Ignoring my obvious bewilderment, the gentleman suddenly began to give a long, long expostulation about Japanese history. Not only was it long, but it contained names of people I had never heard of, and his core line of logic was to weave into history the story of an extremely complex web of interpersonal relationships. What is more, the gentleman carried with him historical materials including genealogical charts that were apparently designed to back up the story he was telling.

"Well, anyway, please come into our office. We will listen to your story." With these words I invited "His Royal Highness" into the building and had everyone listen to his story.

For a while he related a long story about Japanese history that put particular emphasis on the Northern and Southern Courts period. After that he declared, "I am the true Emperor. The present Emperor is a fake." After making this proclamation he made the following request of us, "At the hand of the American military, I wish to be placed in the position of Emperor. And because the present emperor is not the legitimate Emperor, I ask that he be removed from his position."

Frankly speaking, at this time I was not as familiar as I now am with Japanese history, but quite apart from whether his claims were true or not, I thought it was a wonderful and very interesting story.

"General MacArthur should meet with this Emperor Kumazawa," I said, but of course I was half joking. I then asked my superior, Australian Major John Shelton, how I should handle this case.

"We have no choice but to report this matter to the GHQ and leave it to the judgment of General MacArthur." As this was Major Shelton's opinion, we immediately set to work preparing a report to MacArthur's Headquarters. We translated all of the historical materials the gentleman brought with him into English. Among the documents, all of which were written in the most beautiful calligraphy, the core document was a genealogy of the Kumazawa family, which served to show that he was the legitimate Emperor in terms of pedigree.

In the process of the translation work, I had some chances to speak with the man, and I think he was an extremely gentlemanly and very charming person. As I got to know him better, he told me his experiences of persecution during the war. "Before the war, it was not easy to say that I am the legitimate Emperor. The police were always keeping watch on me and they ordered me to be silent. There was nothing I could do to protest this treatment. . . ."

He concluded by saying that after the defeat, since Japan had become free under the direction of the American military, he wanted General MacArthur to hear his original claim.

Of course, his "Imperial Proclamation" became quite a topic of discussion, and, needless to say, it was taken up by a large number of newspapers. The *Stars and Stripes* printed a report on the matter on January 18, 1946, and on the next day the Japanese newspapers reported it. And it was not only the Japanese newspapers; foreign newspapers also reported the matter, making the story suddenly into a matter of international attention.

At ATIS we translated the long story that "Emperor Kumazawa" had told us into English, made up a portfolio to which we attached the historical documents that he gave us, and sent everything to GHQ.

A whole month passed after we had sent up the report, but absolutely no word had been heard. Two months passed, and there was still no word. Finally, with no reply from GHQ, the matter was disposed of quietly. The GHQ completely ignored—or gave the silent treatment to—this whole matter of "Emperor Kumazawa," and no reply was ever forthcoming.

However, if one thinks about it, one must admit that this policy of saying absolutely nothing was actually extremely wise on their part. For as far as GHQ was concerned, they could hardly say "yes," and yet there was no necessity for them to proclaim a conclusion to the matter by saying "no" either. So they simply paid no attention to the matter at all.

For several moths after we sent the documents to the GHQ, "Emperor Kumazawa" came frequently seeking to meet with me in order to ask what General MacArthur's reply had been.

"Has a reply come from General MacArthur? What did he say??"

"GHQ is presently considering this case. They are now researching the question of the Emperor. I have no idea how they are attempting to deal with this question, but it is certain that it is under consideration."

Every time the gentleman visited my office and asked me about the matter, this is how I answered. Or rather, this is how I had no choice but to answer.

At first, the gentleman showed up at my office about once a week to ask about the conclusion. After I repeated the same response over and over, his visits dropped to once every two weeks, then once every three weeks, until finally he stopped coming altogether. It was not until many years later that I heard that he had passed away in 1966.

So this incident ended, in effect, in the defeat of "Emperor Kumazawa." But what really attracted my interest in this matter was when I found out that, even if this sort of "incident" was not totally unprecedented in Japanese history, it was extremely rare. And further, I found out that before the war, this matter was subject to the interference of the police and that those concerned were compelled to keep silent about it. For in Europe, needless to say, even if this sort of thing did not exactly happen all the time, analogous claims were common, and certainly nothing to be regarded as unusual or strange.

In Europe, of course, from ancient times, there have been a great many wars and incessant struggles regarding succession to the throne. Accordingly, among those who were defeated in these struggles, there were often princes who claimed, "It is I who am the rightful successor to the throne!"

"It is I who am the true king!"

"It is I who am the real heir to the throne!"

In England and Holland, not to mention France and other countries, it was not a very difficult thing to find such claimants to the throne.

For a person like me brought up in this Western civilization, the incident of "Emperor Kumazawa" was not something especially new or unusual, much less a "matter of the gravest import that must not be mentioned." It was nothing more than an interesting story. What *was* strange and unusual for me, rather, was the fact that the whole incident was strictly suppressed as a "matter of great import that must not be mentioned," as well as the related fact that this sort of "appeal" was extremely rare in Japan.

Perhaps it is a simple thing to say that this was the effect of the ideology of the single, unbroken imperial line, but one must admit that the spiritual shadow cast upon Japanese society and culture by the Emperor system was great indeed.

14

The Yokohama Court

ONE OF THE THINGS that I remember well about the translation work in this period is the matter of the diaries that were presented as evidence in the Yokohama Court.

The Yokohama Court was the court where the trials of the class B and C war criminals, under the authority of the U.S. Eighth Army, were carried out.

According to Philip R. Piccigallo in his book *The Japanese on Trial*, 309 of the 474 public trials of suspects accused of inhumane treatment of Allied prisoners of war were carried out here. These included the military trial of the suspects in the Ishigaki Island incident, in which American prisoners of war were beheaded, which resulted in the hanging of forty-one Japanese soldiers. There was also the military trial of those involved in the case of the vivisection experiments carried out on eight American prisoners of war at Kyushu Imperial University, where one of the experimenters was said to have dined on the liver of one of the victims.

The case I was involved in as a translator included an incident similar to the vivisection case at Kyushu University. This incident began when, shortly before the end of the war, a B-29 involved in the blanket bombing of Japanese cities was shot down by the Japanese military, and two of the airmen parachuted out and landed in a small mountain village. The airmen, of course, were captured by the inhabitants of the village, who proceeded to behead them, remove their hearts and livers, and cook and eat them. Afterward they stuck the men's heads on the top of poles and displayed them in the central square of the village. Moreover, I forget whether it was the chief of the village or one of his assistants, but in any case a leader of the village had written out the whole incident in detail in his diary.

As a matter of course, immediately after the war an investigation into this incident by the Allied forces began, and as a result, those suspected of responsibility for the murders in the village were brought to the Yokohama Court. And one of the pieces of material evidence that was confiscated at the time of the arrests was the diary of the village leader.

I got involved in this case because I was asked to translate the diary into English. The translation itself was not such a difficult thing. The writer of the diary was a person of some education so the diary was written in very attractive and proper characters, and I had a good supply of dictionaries so there was nothing I had to puzzle about. However, in terms of its content, this work was not a pleasant thing to carry out. The barbarity of the act made me feel very sick to my stomach. "On such-and-such day of the such-and-such month, we beheaded two B-29 airmen . . ." This sort of shocking fact was actually written down in a diary.

The diary that I translated was, needless to say, brought forth as evidence at the time of the trial. As translator, I was required to go to the Yokohama Court to swear that the content of my translation was accurate.

At the court, the judge showed me the diary and the translation, and I was asked to verify its identity and make my oath. "Lieutenant Goodman, is this truly the diary in question?"

"Yes, it certainly is."

"Did you translate this into English?"

"Yes, I did."

"Is the translation accurate?"

"Yes, it is."

That was the whole of my testimony. Since after this interchange I left the courtroom, I have no way of knowing how the trial went or what the result was. But if the record of the trial were to turn up, I am sure that my translation of the diary with my signature on it would be there.

Nevertheless, even now my hair stands on end when I think of the wartime actions of the Japanese that were recorded in this diary. Indeed, I had heard the rumors that during the war, Japanese ate the flesh of POWs. I had already heard that while I was in the Philippines. However, I thought that this sort of thing was a fabrication that was nothing more than propaganda. But through translating this diary, I came to know that the story of Japanese eating human flesh was not a rumor but something based on fact, though that does not mean it was a common occurrence.

I just have one question about all this, and that is, why did Japanese people do such a thing?

Of course, there are lots of stories of people in the East or West being compelled to eat human flesh when faced with imminent starvation. And in a sense, when one considers the extreme circumstances these Japanese were faced with, the occurrence of such "incidents" can arouse a certain amount of sympathy.

Nevertheless, what about this "one incident" recorded in this diary of killing men who had given up their power of resistance as a kind of example or lesson, or as a kind of blood sacrifice like those carried out in ancient times or in tribal societies to bring good luck in battle?

It goes without saying that this incident was born out of the sufferings and inhumanities of war. It is impossible to imagine it happening outside of the special conditions and desperation brought about by warfare.

If one thinks about it, at the time this incident happened, B-29s were flying through the skies of Japan day after day, whenever and wherever they liked, with virtually no resistance. Of course, this mountain village was not a target of bombing attacks, but the cities nearby were being turned into oceans of fire, day after day and night after night. And this fact was being conveyed to this village deep in the mountains, mixed in with propaganda and exaggeration, enflaming the patriotism of the villagers and their enmity toward American soldiers. In these sorts of circumstances, it is not so difficult to understand how such an incident might happen. Truly, the eating of human flesh is something that stretches the limits of one's imagination, and it is an act that exceeds all the limits of morality.

Yet beheading people (*kubikiri*) and *hara-kiri*—whether forced or voluntary—were very common occurrences in fifteenth- and sixteenth-century Japan, and they were not even unusual in the period before and during the Meiji Restoration, just some 135 years ago. If one turns the pages of Japanese history, one reads, for instance, that the great warrior hero of the Warring States period, Oda Nobunaga, used the skulls of his long-term enemies Asai Hisamasa and his son Nagamasa as wine cups to share the New Year's wine with his comrades. And for the samurai, cutting off the heads of one's enemies in battle as trophies of war was an integral part of the traditional Japanese way of warfare. Moreover, the strange custom of committing *seppuku* (*hara-kiri*) in battle, to take responsibility for defeat, though extremely hard for us Westerners to understand, was seen among the Japanese military in the Second World War.

All the same, however one looks at it, the "incident" recorded in this village diary remains an extremely peculiar case. Nevertheless, if we think about it, this sort of incident does not occur all the time, but only in time of war or in the midst of the action of battle. In this sense, before we start putting blame on the Japanese tradition, we must consider warfare itself as the primary factor.

Actually, warfare is something that turns human beings into crazed animals. Not just Japanese, but Americans as well. In chapter 5, "To the Front Lines in the Philippines," I have already made some mention of it, but during World War II American soldiers were extremely reluctant to take Japanese soldiers as prisoners, almost always preferring to kill them instead.

We intelligence officers, or the intelligence service, asked the soldiers on the front line to obtain prisoners for us so we could acquire military information, but they were out for blood and treated these requests with indifference, shooting and killing a great many Japanese soldiers who should have been taken prisoner.

In New Guinea, in the Philippines, and everywhere on the Pacific battlegrounds, Japanese soldiers skillfully disguised themselves and went into hiding in the jungle, shooting and killing American soldiers as they advanced. Battle buddies who had until yesterday, or rather, until just a little while ago, been eating meals together, telling jokes to each other, and developing friendships, would suddenly fall and die. If the American soldiers, filled with anger, discovered a Japanese soldier, without hesitation they would shoot him or torture him to death. And who could criticize them for it? Even if the Japanese soldier was wounded, it was a situation of kill or be killed. There are certainly differences of degree, but wherever there is a battleground you will find this sort of extreme situation.

If nuclear war had broken out between the U.S. and the Soviet Union and I had seen family members, relatives, and close friends killed, and then a Soviet bomber was shot down and two of its crew members parachuted to the ground and landed nearby, I wonder if I myself would have been able to suppress my anger and my desire for revenge, and treat them in a humanitarian way.

15

The Democratic Boom, the English Boom, and the Christianity Boom

IN MERELY TWO or three months after the beginning of the Occupation, three great changes occurred among the Japanese that could not have been imagined before. The first was the study of democracy, the second was the study of English, and the third was the study of Christianity.

To say that the changes occurred overnight would be a bit extreme, but in the twinkling of an eye, like bamboo shoots sprouting up after the rain, private English conversation schools sprang up all over Tokyo. Just how many were there? There is no way to get an accurate count, but there were certainly several hundred of them. And even though so many schools opened, the number of students entering was like an endless stream, and there were almost always lines of applicants stretching out like long snakes in front of the school doors. If so many English conversation schools appeared, there was naturally a drastic jump in the demand for teachers. Immediately there was a shortage, and American servicemen became the logical targets of recruitment. They were not only teachers, but people who could speak the real English of the homeland.

Through a friend's introduction I also became an English teacher. At the time, I was young and had a lot of energy added to a strong sense of curiosity, and what is more, such teaching gave me an ideal chance to speak everyday Japanese with Japanese people. For these reasons I decided eagerly to become a part-time English teacher. Through the same friend's introduction, the first place that I worked as an English teacher was the Japan-America Conversation Academy.

I think that this was one of the first English language schools established after the war. Because I had an introduction, in the daytime I worked for ATIS in the NYK building, teaching at the Academy only in the evenings. I think it was just two evenings a week—Tuesday and Thursday—for two hours each evening. The age of the students ranged very widely, and there were both men and women. For men and women to study together in the same classroom was unimaginable before the war, so the students, who had no experience of "co-education," seemed a little uncomfortable at first. I did not use texts. After a while, the school itself began to prepare mimeographed text-books, but I did not use them.

I discussed democracy with the students, and I wanted to teach them through English conversation what democracy was all about. Of course, I could speak Japanese and wanted to speak Japanese with them, but I resisted the temptation and followed a policy of, in principle, not speaking Japanese at all in the class-room. That was, after all, the best way for them to make progress in their English conversation. However, when they completely failed to understand what I said, I had no choice but to resort at times to a bit of Japanese.

Education in democracy through lessons in English conversation was something that was very popular among the Japanese students. They were eager to discuss this topic, and it seemed that they got a very strong impression of democracy in this way. In addition to that sort of discussion, I prepared lecture notes about topics such as the American election system, the judicial system, regional autonomy, the federal government, American history, and philosophy, talking to them about these things in easy-to-understand English.

In preparing these lecture notes, I bought and studied Japanese books about American political history, such as Imai Toshiki's *Beikokushi* (A History of America). Accordingly, I don't think the students did any preparation for class at all. I would move around the class and name each student individually, then ask a question which was to be answered in English. Of course, using the blackboard I noted down the important topics of discussion for each class.

I think this style of running the class was popular with the students. They eagerly answered my questions, and the atmosphere in the classroom was very lively. Often they would find appropriate opportunities to give me gifts, like rice cakes, decorative wrapping cloths (*furoshiki*), obis, Japanese dolls, and so on.

It was still not long since the end of the war, and there was an extreme shortage of resources, so for them to give me such gifts was no easy thing. Of course, I was happy to receive them, and I have carefully kept the obis and *furoshiki* and dolls, if not the rice cakes, as mementos.

For the students to give me presents in this way was perhaps their own way of expressing their gratitude to me, as a *gaijin*, for my efforts and my manner of teaching. To look a little deeper, though, I think that although the scale and the purposes of gift-giving were very different, there was something in the psychology behind the act that was of the very same nature as that which motivated the giving of gifts to MacArthur.

And I did not only *teach* at the Japan-America Conversation Academy. There was also a great deal that the students taught me. For, through my conversations with them in English, I was able to learn about many aspects of their lives both during and after the war. The conversations always began something like this:

"Where do you live?"

"What kind of work do you do?"

"What kind of place is it that you work?"

So many questions immediately elicited a variety of information about their daily lives.

"My home (or office, etc.) was destroyed by fire" (. . . *ga yakechatta*).

This was the first "new Japanese" that I learned at the Academy. From this the reader should be able to imagine to some extent what sort of topics we discussed in our English conversation lessons.

I think there was no word that more precisely captured the reality of Japan right after the end of the war than *yakechatta* and the closely connected word, the "ruins of a burned-out building" (*yakeato*). As mentioned before, virtually all of the buildings of Tokyo had been burned down in the air raids, so that only "*yakeato*" remained. I think that now *yakeato* has become a dead word, or something close to a dead word, in contemporary Japan. On the subject of "dead words," another that comes to mind is "Metropolitan tramcar," or "streetcar" (*toden*).

In the early 1980s there was only one streetcar still in operation that had not yet been removed, which ran between Minowa and Waseda. Right after the war we loved to take the Metropolitan tramcar wherever we were going. At the time, if one used the word "electric train" (*densha*), it referred normally to the

Metropolitan tramcar, which literally served the role of the "feet" of the residents of Tokyo in those days. Of course, it is not that there were no buses at the time, but with the acute shortage of gasoline, they had to rely mostly on the charcoal-burning bus of the wartime period, which carried a big cauldron on the back, and the number of these busses was extremely small.

In connection with the word *densha* (streetcar), I have a very strong memory from my days at the Japan-American Conversation Academy. It was a story that a certain woman told me about something that happened during the war. To reproduce her story:

It was something that happened on a certain day during the war on a densha.

An army officer dressed in full uniform and carrying his weapons boarded the tram. But no one in the tram paid any attention to him, because they were all exhausted from the war.

The soldier looked around the tram, but no one looked in his direction, everyone just sitting there silently looking down. At the sight of this total lethargy, the soldier suddenly became very angry, and started yelling at everyone, "Attention! Stand up!"

But no one made a move.

He became angrier and angrier and continued to shout, "You are all traitors! You are a disgrace to the Japanese people! Can't you hear the orders of His Majesty, the Emperor??"

When he saw that, even now, no one made a move, he got off the tram at the next stop.

After telling me this story slowly in very laborious English, the woman added, "We were exhausted. We were truly broken by the war. So no one wanted to do anything. We just wanted to be still and quiet."

THE DEMOCRATIC BOOM, THE ENGLISH BOOM, AND THE CHRISTIANITY BOOM

In the classroom at the Japan-America Conversation Academy, I wondered why and to whom she had told this story. Was the story directed to me, to her friends in the class, or to herself? And did she tell the story to demonstrate that she was not a "war criminal"? I don't know which it was, and there is no way that I can ascertain it now.

Whichever it was, it was a story that stimulated one's curiosity, and I don't think that the story itself was untrue. I imagine that she probably directed the story to me, that is, to a soldier in the Occupation army. She must have wanted to describe how much ordinary Japanese citizens suffered during the war, both in material deprivation and in the loss of individual freedom.

Regarding the topic of English conversation and democracy at the Japan-America Conversation Academy, there was something else I discovered, which I continue to believe even now: The students at the Academy showed a strong interest in democracy and asked me all kinds of questions, but these were mostly about the number of elected representatives in Congress, their functions, and the mechanisms by which Congress operates—in other words, questions about the political system itself. Questions about what sort of historical background and what sort of ideas or philosophical foundation gave rise to this system were extremely rare. In fact, they were nonexistent. This was true not only of the students at the Japan-American Conversation Academy, but I think it was true of all of the Japanese people with whom I discussed this sort of topic at the time.

To speak a little boldly just on the basis of my impression, I would say that their way of thinking was something like this:

There was a great defect in the Japanese political organization and the Emperor system before the war. Because of that, Japan lost the war. The American mode of political organization and democracy is far superior. Therefore they won the war. Accordingly, it is necessary for us to learn that system.

The language that is used by democratic people and those who promote democracy, like General MacArthur, is English. We must respect and learn the three "sacred regalia" that lay behind America's victory—democracy, English, and the U.S. political system.

Perhaps people like me who, as Occupation soldiers, used English at the Academy to teach about democracy, also became objects of this kind of "respect." Even though I received no fan letter "attacks" like MacArthur, the fact that, like him, I was honored by being showered with gifts does not seem totally unconnected to this sort of psychology on the part of the Japanese.

Be that as it may, as I have described, the Japanese showed a strong interest in the *system* of democracy. But as Professor Robert Ward of Stanford University often pointed out, there actually is quite a difference between the democratic *system* and the philosophy or ideals of democracy. Both MacArthur and the Japanese, without becoming aware of this difference, somehow believed that once a democratic system was set firmly in place, the philosophy of democracy would automatically arise.

Truly, in the period between 1945 and 1946, in an American kind of way, the philosophy of democracy *was* present as a kind of wind blowing in the air, but I think the Japanese of the time were far too ignorant of the long and trouble-filled history behind the development of democratic thought and democratic systems in the West.

Nevertheless, for more than half a century since the end of the war, the constitutional system established after the war—

though going through its share of twists and turns—has managed somehow to maintain itself. This fact in itself has its own share of historical reasons: One is the fact that the fifty years or so of dark history under the Meiji Constitutional system has remained in people's memories. Another is the fact that people with culture and education continue to work hard to maintain the best things in Japan's historical and cultural tradition. And another is the fact that after the Occupation there was a long period of robust economic growth. However, I do not think that because of this relative longevity one can jump to the conclusion that Japanese culture and society have really accepted and fostered the philosophy of democracy. I still retain the fear that an even greater test still lies ahead for democracy in Japan.

In addition to English conversation and democracy, another cultural phenomenon that flowered after the war was Christianity. Some Japanese today can undoubtedly still remember attending church or Sunday school in their youth. I am sure that many can also remember smacking their lips enjoying the oranges given out through the churches. Yes, there actually was a period when the U.S. distributed oranges through the churches, and at a time of vitamin shortages these gifts were warmly welcomed by the Japanese. There were long lineups of people winding around the churches waiting for their oranges.

And there was, so to speak, a kind of "Christianity boom," and it became widely known that even the Emperor himself was studying the Bible. As in the case of the study of democracy and English, perhaps one could also say the basic way of thinking behind the 'Christianity boom" was the idea that:

Before the war there were great defects in Shinto and Buddhism, and for that reason we lost the war. The Christianity of the West is much superior, and that is why they won the war. Thus we must also study Christianity.

And the person who embodied all of these three symbols of victory in one body was none other than the Supreme Commander of the Allied Powers, General Douglas MacArthur.

16

Two Suicides

THOUGH IT IS A different topic, I would like here to relate two
unhappy events that occurred within the Occupation army during the period I was living in the NYK Building and working
with ATIS.

I suppose that armies in any country, whether past or present, are rational organizations whose purpose is to win wars,
and therefore they must reject waste of all kinds and have no
room to give consideration to the feelings of the individual.
However, as a result, the solution to the excesses and frictions to
which this gives rise are all sought within the individual so that
certain people often end up suffering in the extreme. For this
reason, suicides occur.

While I was working in the NYK Building, there were two
significant suicides. One was a second-generation Japanese-
American sergeant who was my own subordinate, and the
other was a classmate from my days at the Army Japanese

Language School who worked as an intelligence officer in another section.

I will begin with the sergeant. This man was an extremely quiet fellow who was often alone, and it seemed that he did not have any especially close friends. However, he was talented and much trusted by his co-workers, and he handled things very conscientiously and thoroughly. Accordingly, when he was at work he was always plugging away intently and silently. If I asked him something, he would answer very politely, but he rarely said anything on his own accord.

One day a soldier came rushing into my room all blue in the face. "Lieutenant Goodman, come right away! Something awful has happened to the sergeant!"

Wondering what on earth had happened, in a great rush I ran out of my room and followed the soldier up to the fourth floor. On the fourth floor there was a hall where we often had parties, and on the side of the hall there was a small utility room containing a water heater, a gas stove, and various kitchen utensils.

The soldier pointed into this utility room, and I saw the second-generation Japanese sergeant lying there collapsed with no color in his face. The room was full of gas, and the smell was overwhelming. From this it was immediately clear that he had released gas throughout the utility room and committed suicide. We stood there in shock for several seconds, but then came to our senses and called a doctor. We did everything possible to revive him, but it was too late—he was already gone. I think he was only twenty-six or twenty-seven at the time—so young.

Why did he commit suicide? No one had the slightest idea. As I mentioned he was a quiet and solitary kind of guy, not the type who would directly divulge his feelings, and he seemed to have no close friends to whom he could confide his feelings anyway.

Nevertheless, I wanted to find out the reason. Otherwise I just could not come to grips with myself. He was, after all, a talented subordinate who was working together with me. After doing some investigation, I found out that the sergeant's family was from Hiroshima, and that they had emigrated from Hiroshima to the U.S. in his father's generation. When his parents found out that he was coming to Japan as a soldier in the army, they urged him to go to Hiroshima and see his relatives, and he wanted very much to do so himself. If he went to Hiroshima, he could see his mother's brothers and sisters—before he set off for Hiroshima, he had reportedly said this to everyone. So, taking advantage of a weekend break, he boldly traveled to Hiroshima to visit his relatives.

The result was horrifying. As the world knows, it was not long after the atomic bomb had been dropped on Hiroshima, and the whole city was in ruins. What the sergeant found out from visiting Hiroshima was that most of his relatives had been killed in the bombing. Those that survived, I heard, not only did not welcome him when he came, but cursed him and yelled at him at the top of their voices,"You are not our relative! You are the enemy! Aren't you wearing the uniform of the American military? Didn't you people murder our uncles and aunts? You are a murderer! Get the hell out of here! I never want to speak to you again!"

When he came back to Tokyo, he became even more silent and solitary than before, and it seems he sank into a deep depression. However, since he had always been a man of few words, his condition did not draw very many people's attention.

His suicide followed shortly thereafter.

I have described the change in his state of mind here on the basis of my own understanding of what I heard from his friends and acquaintances. While the minor details may involve some conjecture on my part, the overall picture, I am sure, is quite accurate.

I will now talk about the other colleague who committed suicide.

As I already mentioned, he was my classmate in the same graduating class as mine at the Army Japanese Language School. He was a Jewish refugee from Germany who came to the U.S. in 1938 or 1939. As is well known, this is the time when the Nazi persecution of Jews was becoming more and more severe, and many Jews were trying to get out of Germany. He was one of those who managed to get out.

He later got interested in Japanese, enlisted in the army, and studied Japanese together with me, eventually landing in Japan together with the rest of us military intelligence officers. He was a sincere man who was also very intelligent. And he also was living, like me, in the NYK Building.

One day, he answered a phone call from someone. No one paid any mind at the time, but even now I remember him saying over and over, "No. I can't do it. I can't do it. It is out of the question. I can't do it." After he hung up and came back to where we were, he was still angry.

"What's the matter?" we asked.

"Ah, it's nothing. Don't worry about it," he said, unwilling to take us into his confidence.

I think it was two or three weeks later that we found him in his bed dead, having shot himself with his pistol. Normally we did not carry guns. Since ATIS members basically did not participate directly in hostilities, we normally did not possess guns. However, about a week, I think, after that mysterious phone call I noticed that he had a gun.

"Hey, you, what are you up to?" I asked suspiciously.

"I am cleaning my gun."

"Why are you cleaning your gun at a time like this?"

To my persistent questioning I think he just answered, "Hmm. I don't really know. I just feel like cleaning my gun."

About a week later, he proclaimed,

"I am going to commit suicide."

To this we responded, "Is that guy joking?"

If your own friend were to say, "I am going to commit suicide," I think most people would not take it seriously, but would probably say something like, "Stop your bad jokes and forget it. Forget it." But a week after he made his proclamation, he put his gun to his temple and fired.

Why on earth would he commit suicide?

As in the previous case, I did my best to find out what the reason was by asking his friends and acquaintances. First, as for the phone call that started the whole thing, the call came from Sugamo Prison. At the time, Sugamo Prison held a large number of suspected war criminals who were designated as class A war criminals. Along with the highest-ranking Japanese war leaders, led by Tōjō Hideki, there were also high-ranking officials of Japan's allies, Germany and Italy, who had been stationed in Japan, and were now under arrest and surveillance. The Germans held were Nazi diplomats, most prominently the German ambassador to Japan during the war, Ott. And German-speaking individuals were needed to conduct the interrogation of these prisoners.

So it was on my German Jewish friend that the white-feathered arrow landed. He spent his childhood in Germany and his youth in America, and now he was in Japan as a military intelligence officer. The judgment of the bigwigs in the army must have been that there was no one better qualified to interrogate the Nazi officials.

Needless to say, he refused this request. And for one

simple reason,"I don't ever want to see the faces of those Nazi characters."

It is not difficult to imagine how much he hated the Nazis. It was the anti-Jewish policy of the Nazis that had driven him from his native land in the first place, and it was now known that over six million Jews were sent to the gas chambers in the concentration camps. If he were to meet these people in the position of an official interpreter during their questioning, could one expect him to be able to carry out the translation in a normal state of mind?

Nevertheless, the military top brass ordered him to go to Sugamo Prison and carry out the questioning of the Nazis. For an intelligence officer in ATIS whose main duties were translation and interpretation, what grounds did he have for refusing such an order? To follow orders or to follow one's own feelings. Damned if you do and damned if you don't. Not so different from the famous theme of Edo literature and drama: do I follow *giri* (duty) or follow *ninjō* (one's true nature)?

Through the method of taking his own life, a method well known in the Japanese tradition as well, he pronounced his "solution" to this impossible dilemma. As a close friend of his, I wondered how the news of his suicide could best be conveyed to his parents. At his funeral, anger and sorrow about his death welled up from deep within me, and I could not hold back my tears.

When I visited Japan thirty years later in 1975, wishing to pay my respects at his grave, I visited the foreigners' cemetery in Yokohama where he was buried. I searched for his grave, and although thirty years had passed, I searched for it by following my memory. Yet it could not be found. I could not even find his name in the list of foreigners buried in the foreigners' cemetery. I think his remains were probably removed to the U.S., but now there is no way to find out for sure.

My Trip to Shanghai

I HAVE ALREADY described how terrible the situation was in Japan right after the war in terms of supplies of food, clothing, and housing. To look back on it now, the terrible living conditions in Japan at the time really exceeded one's ability to imagine. Accordingly, the officers and men of the Occupation army had no choice but to spend most of their time in the barracks to which they were assigned, without any real entertainment. Of course going out in the evening to see a movie or a play or something else was inconceivable.

If we wanted to enjoy our holidays (Rest and Recuperation) in a leisurely way, we had no choice but to go outside of Japan, and American military personnel, or the officers at least, were allowed to take about a week's vacation in a region outside Japan after working for a certain period of time in the Occupation army.

In my case, I got my vacation in the spring of 1946, and spent my week in Shanghai, China. I left from Atsugi Airfield in

Kanagawa Prefecture aboard a small twin-engine military aircraft called the C-47, the same model as a DC-3. The plane was full of American officers who were also heading to Shanghai for their vacations. Since this was a propeller-driven plane, it took over five hours to fly non-stop to Shanghai.

Shanghai at the end of the war had suffered infinitely less destruction than Tokyo, and the city was more beautiful and bustling than I can express. Supplies of food and so on were also plentiful. Of course, this is not to say that the city had not been influenced by the war. Shanghai before the war was an international city, and, as is well known, it contained British, French, and other foreign concession areas. When the war between Japan and China broke out in July 1937, the Japanese occupied the Chinese city but not the foreign concessions. But when the Pacific War broke out in December 1941, they also occupied the foreign concessions. Nevertheless, because the battles between the Japanese and the Chinese armies occurred mostly in the suburbs, the city itself remained almost without damage. The hotels were untouched, the fashionable shops were intact, and there were no scars of war in the city.

The preservation of Shanghai's former appearance was not limited just to this period; when I visited the city again in 1982 with a friend, I felt there had still been no drastic change. My friend and I were able to find streets and alleyways that looked exactly the same as they had in 1946.

When I went from Atsugi in the spring of 1946, I walked from the Shanghai airport to a then upscale hotel called the Cathay Mansions and rented a room as the "base" for my vacation. The hotel had been built in the 1920s and was known through the 1920s and 1930s as one of Shanghai's best hotels. After the Revolution only the name was changed, and it still stands today as the Peace Hotel.

The year 1946 was still on the eve of the Chinese Revolution, and Shanghai had just recently been returned to Chinese Nationalist sovereignty. Accordingly, the prewar foreign concessions retained their foreign atmosphere, and a lot of foreigners were still living there. There were British, French, white Russians who had fled the 1917 Bolshevik Revolution, and refugees from Europe, mostly Jews who had fled from Germany and Austria. The historical circumstances that had brought people of so many races and nationalities here were as varied as one can imagine—a veritable microcosm of the turbulent history of the first half of the twentieth century. So I enjoyed my week's vacation in a Shanghai that still retained the atmosphere of the foreign concessions.

Shanghai in the spring of 1946 . . . I feel that the Shanghai of that time had two completely different "faces." One face was the rich and luxurious Shanghai. Wealthy Chinese and expatriates lived in beautiful homes, had lots of servants, bought all kinds of luxury items, and truly lived a gorgeous life. The other face was that of a city in the throes of horrendous inflation. The common inhabitants of the city were truly in dire straits trying desperately to cope with a daily rise in the prices of commodities. The severity of the inflation was something beyond the imagination of those born after the war. In fact, it is probably unimaginable even to those older Japanese who experienced the inflation in Japan right after the end of the war. The severity of China's inflation was far, far greater than that of Japan, and comparable to that experienced in Germany in the Weimar Republic after the First World War.

For the value of the paper money issued by the KMT (Kuomintang) Nationalist government kept dropping without limit, so that even to buy a few little things or have a meal one had to pay an astronomical amount of paper money. I don't remember the exact figures, but it cost something like three million yuan for a meal, and about four million yuan for a carton of cigarettes.

Every time we went to buy something, we had to stuff bags full of Nationalist Government notes, and fork over great piles of them as payment. To carry my bags of money, I had to hire a Chinese youth especially for the job, and have him follow me through the street wherever I went. Since a whole bag of money was not worth very much, one was not much afraid of thieves, but the heaviness and size of the bags and the troublesomeness of making payments were really irritating. Yet even in the midst of such horrendous inflation, strangely enough, people would not stop using paper money. Thus, what people carried around with them was still unmistakably paper money, and not just toilet paper. In fact, in the hotel we exchanged U.S. dollars for Nationalist Government paper money, but it was extremely dangerous to exchange money at the black-market money changers on the street, for the notes were made cheaply, and it was extremely easy to make counterfeit notes.

The reader may already be able to imagine what it was like to go shopping or eat in restaurants in such a situation, but let me attempt to describe it. First one would walk into an attractive restaurant. Since Chinese cuisine was the standard local fare, one went instead to French restaurants, Viennese restaurants, German restaurants, Russian restaurants, and so on. Unlike Tokyo at the time, Shanghai was full of excellent restaurants, so every day and every evening I had my fill of the best cuisines from all over the world. If I had Viennese food for lunch, I would have Russian food for dinner, and for the next day's lunch I would have French food, and then German food for dinner. Every day was a new experience and a new enjoyment. The bill would be as much as six million yuan. Sometimes it was seven million. And there were even times when it went as high as eight million. My Chinese money-bag porter would open the money bag upon my instructions and pay the bill with bundles of bank notes. The cashier would confirm the amount and receive it. Feeling satisfied, gustatorily and financially, I would leave the restaurant.

Not only did I enjoy my meals in Shanghai, but I also saw a lot of movies. Shanghai had been occupied, in effect, by the Japanese military for eight years, from 1937 to 1945, during which time Japanese movies, but no American movies, had been shown. The residents of Shanghai must have been starved for American movies, for as soon as the Japanese surrendered and the city was returned to KMT administration, all of the movie houses immediately started screening American movies from the 1930s and 1940s.

Shanghai's nightclubs were also fantastic. In the evenings, taking along my money-bag porter, I would go to a nightclub and enjoy myself watching the show. Here I was able to enjoy high-class prewar English Scotch and famous-name American cigarettes ("Lucky Strike Green") that I hadn't seen since the beginning of the war. This was because in the period of Japanese occupation, under the controlled economy, such items that escaped into the black market were hidden away in the back of warehouses and never released onto the market. With Japan's surrender and the abandonment of economic controls, these products flowed out into the market like water after the breaking of a dike. Famous brands of alcohol and tobacco, high-class chocolate; all sorts of luxury items were flooding the market in Shanghai at this time.

What is more, we American officers were given the warmest of welcomes in the former foreign concessions of Shanghai, and were invited to people's homes and showered with kindnesses. One by one, they invited each of us to their homes and did everything to make us comfortable in gratitude for our labors. I remember that some of the men so entertained fell in love with girls they met at the homes they were invited to, got married, and returned to the U.S. with brides from Shanghai.

The home I was invited to for dinner was that of a white Russian family. The atmosphere of the home was very elegant, and the house itself was truly beautiful and equipped with furniture and appliances to match, including a magnificent large kettle for making tea called a samovar, a luxury item much loved by the Russians. They entertained me with a multi-course home-cooked meal that was superb beyond belief.

"You are our great benefactors who saved us from the oppressive rule of the Japanese. Don't hesitate to visit us anytime. You will always be welcome!" They said this sort of thing repeatedly and treated me with the greatest attentiveness and respect.

My week in Shanghai was full of such enjoyable memories. Shanghai at peace. In such a Shanghai there was no way one could feel any clear signs of the coming storms of revolution that were to engulf the city three years later. Of course, the civil war between the KMT and the Communists had already begun, but the battles between them had not reached Shanghai, and the influence of the Communist Party had, on the surface at least, not yet reached the city.

But this was truly only on the surface, for underneath the signs of the coming revolution were gradually manifesting themselves, and even a short-term visitor such as me caught wind of all kinds of stories about the corruption of KMT officials. That corruption itself, it seems, was gradually beginning to bring the influence of the Communist Party into the city's administration.

However, although I did not think that the corruption of the

KMT government officials was a good thing, I felt that, to a degree, it was inevitable. For they had been driven by the Japanese occupation into rural districts where supplies were scarce, and they had held on there for eight years, keeping up the struggle without surrendering. The hardship they had gone through was at least as bad as that suffered by the American army during the Pacific War. In that case, if, after they returned to the city, they sought some "extra salary" as compensation for their eight years of hardship, could anyone really blame them? Of course, I am not saying that the corruption of the high KMT government officials should be regarded with approval, but just that, in the year after the termination of Japanese military administration, I felt that it could not be just condemned out of hand.

Even though the city's appearance on the surface was unchanged, in its foundations Shanghai had witnessed an epochal transition, and it was soon to see another one. I think that the people who felt this the most sharply were the foreigners living in the foreign concessions. The residents of the foreign concessions expected, or rather were convinced, that Shanghai was going to return sooner or later to complete Chinese control, whether under the KMT or the Communist Party, and in order to be ready to escape they wanted to change their paper money and assets in their possession into U.S. dollars. "Would you change government bank notes into U.S. dollars for me?" I was often asked, and I trusted them, so, when asked, I readily agreed to the exchange.

During my stay in Shanghai I heard quite often stories of life under the Japanese occupation: One day a Japanese soldier knocked on the door of a private house, forced his way in, and shot all the inhabitants with a pistol. This kind of thing happened suddenly, without any warning or sign, and without any prior notification. It was like a great pack of murderous ghosts had been let loose in the city. I need hardly say how terrified the city's residents were. All the foreign concession residents I spoke to said without exception that, during the war, "The Japanese were unpredictable; one never knew what they would do next." For this reason they lived in constant fear.

For instance, one day a Japanese soldier would be grinning and laughing cheerfully, but the next day he would be waving his pistol around. And no one would have any idea why. If this sort of thing happens all the time, like the Japanese proverb, "If you don't touch the god, there will be no curse," the residents of the foreign concessions kept their distance from the areas where the Japanese lived, and quickly fled from any place where it looked like they would meet a Japanese. Because of this, the normal hustle and bustle of the city died down, and people tended to stay at home.

Then suddenly came an order from the newly appointed regional commander, "The residents of all quarters are to come out of their homes immediately and line up to be inspected by junior officers. While the officers are making their rounds, everyone must salute them!" Perhaps the new commander who had just taken over from his predecessor wanted to establish his authority by coercing the residents. At any rate, whenever there was a change in the person in command, the temperament of the new commander would take precedence over any rules, and erratic and arbitrary orders would be issued that were not welcomed by the residents. A good example was the treatment of the Jewish refugees in the Shanghai district. One commander, trying to please the Nazis, had them concentrated together in ghettos, while his successor abandoned the policy on the grounds that they were citizens of an allied country.

I heard this sort of story until my ears got sore, but let me add that there was also a story that was an exception to the rule. A certain Jewish refugee girl from a foreign concession told me:

Since it was when the Japanese were occupying the foreign concessions, it must have been in the middle of the Pacific War. One day, suddenly, a knock on the door echoed through the whole house. In an instant everyone in the house froze. A Japanese soldier was standing outside the door.

"We opened the door in trepidation, and we saw a naval officer standing there."

"I heard the sound of a piano," he said to her in English. She was an amateur musician, and the soldier probably heard her playing the piano. Afraid he was going to confiscate her precious piano, she answered, "No, that's not possible. We have no piano in the house." "No, I really heard the sound of a piano. You must have one. Let me have a look around."

When he came into the house it was immediately apparent that there was a piano in one corner. Breaking into a big smile, he sat down in front of the piano and started to play. From then on virtually every day this navy officer would visit the house and throw himself into playing the piano with great gusto.

The girl, who was very wary at first, came to understand that the only purpose of the officer's visit was to play the piano, and she was eventually even playing duets with him.

. . . One day after several weeks had passed, the officer was playing the piano as usual, but when he was finished, he said in English,

"Tomorrow I have to transfer to the front. I really thank you for letting me have so much enjoyment playing your piano! I pray that luck will be with you."

Of course no one, including the girl, had any idea what became of the officer after that.

The Pacific War was rife with killing, rape, and all sorts of inhuman and inhumane behavior. But in the Shanghai foreign concession there was this sort of exceptional Japanese officer.

The Mikado

As I touched upon when relating the story of Emperor Kumazawa, in the eyes of us *gaijin*, the Emperor system was about the strangest and hardest thing in the world at the time to understand. The first time I saw the Emperor was during the year after the end of the war, that is, around January of 1946. The place was the entrance of the National Diet Building. An extremely old-fashioned Daimler limousine stopped at the entrance of the Diet Building, and the Emperor appeared from within. I saw the Emperor very closely when he got out of the car. He was a little smaller than I had expected, and I seem to recall that he was wearing a suit that did not seem to fit him at all, and a strange hat. At first glance he looked a lot like Charlie Chaplin. He had come to the Diet Building to make the proclamation of the opening of the Diet, which is what I had come to see myself. From the observation gallery, this was the first time I heard the Emperor give a speech.

Incidentally, as many of my readers will know, the beginning of 1946 was the time the Emperor made his proclamation that he was human, and not divine. "I am not a god, but a human being." After this proclamation he embarked on an Imperial tour around the country. For us, however, both this "proclamation" and this "Imperial tour of the country" were matters beyond the scope of our understanding.

"Why does a god say things like, 'I am not a god'?"

"If this can't be called a joke, then I don't know what can."

This is the kind of conversation that went on among my comrades.

I said "among my comrades" because, as this was also the policy of General MacArthur, we could not say such things in public. After all, I guess the Emperor was thought to be necessary for the Allied Occupation policy to be carried out smoothly, and to that extent he was "a being of great value." All the same, those in the Allied forces who could speak Japanese were satisfied to use the familiar terms that the ordinary Japanese used to refer to him, "*tenchan*" ("little Emperor") or "*o-tenchan*" ("honorable little Emperor"), and we did not use a term of respect appropriate to such a "being of great value."

In a sense, perhaps this was something quite natural. I can understand what the bigwigs in MacArthur's GHQ thought, but to the officers and soldiers in the Allied forces, until only half a year earlier, he had been one of the supreme leaders of the war on the enemy side, alongside Hitler and Mussolini, and we believed that there was no way he could escape becoming an A-class war criminal.

Due to the changes in the political situation after the war, however, he was removed from the category of those who could be prosecuted as war criminals, but that does not mean that such a high-level political decision was something that could be easily accepted by us ordinary officers and soldiers. Was it not we who fought on the front lines, dodging an endless rain of bullets? I think that the feelings of the Allied officers and soldiers were expressed in our habit of referring to the Emperor as *tenchan* and in the rumors about him that floated around. Moreover, when it came to the Emperor's "Imperial tour of the country," I read about it every day in the newspaper in connection with my work, and I cannot but say that it was something strange.

In order to prove that "the Emperor is a human being," Hirohito "walked" the length and breadth of the land. But to look at it in retrospect, I think his tour was amazingly similar to Truman's traveling all over the U.S. by train in 1948 saying, "I am a candidate for the Presidency." Compared to "I am a candidate for the Presidency," though, I must admit that as a twentieth-century political phenomenon, "the Emperor is a human being" did seem a little ridiculous, a little like a remnant from a distant age.

Shortly after the beginning of the Occupation, the British operetta *The Mikado* was put on at the Takarazuka Theatre, which was renamed the "Ernie Pyle Theatre." The fact that it was performed seems obviously to have been connected to the Emperor—heretofore defined as "divine and inviolable"—making the proclamation that he was only human. Ernie Pyle was an American war correspondent who was killed in the midst of the Battle of Okinawa on Ie Island, and to commemorate him after the war, the Occupation authorities named this confiscated theater after him.

The Mikado is an extremely popular operetta, written in 1885 by the British composer Sir Arthur Sullivan and the British lyricist W. S. Gilbert. It is set in the fictional Japanese town of Titipu, but, though the story is set in Japan, it is actually a satire on the British government of the time.

The first act supposedly takes place in fifteenth-century Japan at the official residence of Ko-Ko in the imaginary town of Titipu. Ko-Ko is a social upstart who has risen from the position of cheap tailor to the position of Lord High Executioner. Then there is Nanki-Poo, the traveling minstrel, who appears in this act. The minstrel is actually the son of the Mikado, the holder of absolute power. Disgusted with his intended marriage to the elderly and ugly Katisha, a female official of the Mikado, he leaves the palace to become a wandering minstrel. Then on his journey Nanki-Poo encounters the attractive girl Yum-Yum and falls in love with her, but he finds out that she is already betrothed to her guardian Ko-Ko.

Suddenly a letter arrives for Ko-Ko from the Mikado. "Has there not been even one execution in the town of Titipu for a whole year? If no execution is carried out in the next month, I will dismiss Ko-Ko from the position of Lord High Executioner on the grounds of neglect of duty."

Ko-Ko discovers Nanki-Poo about to commit suicide because he is so heartbroken about the hopelessness of his love for Yum-Yum. He points out that suicide is a capital offense and offers to do the job professionally. Nanki-Poo agrees, on the condition that he can marry Yum-Yum and enjoy one month of married life before he is beheaded. After the execution Ko-Ko will then be able to marry the widowed Yum-Yum. Ko-Ko has conceived a plot whereby he can kill two birds with one stone, fulfilling the Mikado's command while at the same time eliminating his rival in love. Amidst the celebrations, in storms Katisha, having tracked down the object of her affections, Nanki-Poo, and threatens to reveal his true identity. But she is out-shouted by a chorus of nonsense Japanese syllables: "*O ni! Bikkuri shakkuri to!*" (which translates something like, "So surprised, we hiccup! Bah!")

The second act takes place at the same locale, Ko-Ko's official residence. Just as Nanki-Poo's and Yum-Yum's married life is about to begin, the Mikado and his entourage arrive in Titipu. Ko-Ko sets up his henchmen as his witnesses and reports deceitfully that an execution has already been carried out. The reason the Mikado has come to Titipu with his attendant, Katisha, is because he has heard that his son is there, going under the name of Nanki-Poo. But, horror of horrors, Ko-Ko shows him a certificate of execution on which the name of the executed is given as Nanki-Poo.

Ko-Ko goes to find Nanki-Poo and begs him to present himself, alive, to his father, thereby absolving him of his death, but Nanki-Poo is afraid of Katisha's wrath. Unless Ko-Ko himself will agree to marry the old hag, he declares that he and Yum-Yum will leave on their honeymoon at once. Katisha, meanwhile, is mourning the death of Nanki-Poo. Ko-Ko tries desperately to woo her, but he is at first reluctant. Eventually, however, he wins the formidable lady with a pack of flattering lies and a sad, lovelorn song. Now it comes to light that Nanki-Poo is still alive and married to Yum-Yum. Ko-Ko and Katisha also get married, and the Mikado, though a little bewildered by it all, pronounces that, "Nothing could possibly be more satisfactory!"

In Victorian England, in 1885, around the same time that a popular "Japan village" was built for an exposition in London, this operetta became a great hit. It was performed continually for almost two years, for a total of 672 times, making it one of the most popular—maybe *the* most popular—operettas of all time.

It appears that Gilbert and Sullivan, in the process of writing their operetta, had a very hard time trying to find out things about Japan at a time when the country was virtually unknown.

They wanted to use Japanese-made costumes as much as possible, and they learned about the "manners and behavior of the Japanese" by observing the actions of two Japanese entertainers—a man and a woman—who were performing at the Japan village. How do Japanese men and women walk? How can one express anger by using a fan? How does one express a vow between a lord and a vassal through the use of a fan?

In addition, through a friend, A. B. Mitford, who had the experience of working in the British legation in Tokyo, Sullivan learned the Japanese words "*Miyasama*" (a respectful term of address for members of the Imperial family), as well as "*bikkuri*" (to be surprised) and "*shakkuri*" (to hiccup). He used a chorus singing "Miyasama, miyasama," (Oh noble prince) in the operetta, and, as we have seen above, he used *bikkuri* and *shakkuri* together nonsensically in the same phrase. In this way, the composers somehow tried to create a Japanese atmosphere. Needless to say, however, there were a lot of points in which they were off the mark.

For instance, the characters have ridiculous names like Ko-Ko, Nanki-Poo, and Yum-Yum, which are a sort of English onomatopoeic words, and the location is an imaginary place called Titipu. As one can guess from these names, the atmosphere that is produced on the stage is more like some sort of 19th-century Oriental dream country than Japan.

However, I think this is quite natural. For Gilbert and Sullivan, after all, were borrowing the theme of Japan—or an imaginary image of Japan—to critique or satirize domestic British political problems and the customs and manners of the English people in the Victorian age. Thus, Gilbert and Sullivan both made a point of depicting the "Mikado," appearing on the stage in his royal palanquin, as a strange and comical figure, his entrance accompanied by the chorus singing, "Miya-san, Miya-san!

What is that thing fluttering in front of your horse? *Tokoton yare tonyare na.*"

Needless to say, an operetta that made fun of the Japanese Emperor in such a way was never performed in prewar Japan. If it had been, without doubt the producer of the show would have been thrown into prison on a charge of *lèse-majesté*. Already in 1888, when *The Mikado* had just opened in London, the Japanese ambassador to England became extremely nervous, and on the grounds that the story was set in Japan and expressed "disrespect" for the Japanese Emperor, he petitioned the government to terminate the production. Of course his protest was not accepted. On the contrary, ever since its first performance, the work has been greatly loved by worldwide audiences, and, as mentioned above, in its first production it played continuously for almost two years.

Nevertheless, I think that the British government probably paid some heed to the ambassador's objections, and in 1907, while a member of the Imperial family, Fushimi-no-miya, was visiting England for a period of six weeks, in order to avoid making him feel uncomfortable, the staging of the operetta was prohibited.

In 1907, under the Anglo-Japanese alliance, Japan had become an important and indispensable ally of Great Britain, and it was also the time when Japan was fast consolidating its position as the dominant power in East Asia, due to its victory over Russia in 1905.

Thirty-eight years later, by contrast, when the tables were turned, Japan had lost the Pacific War, and the U.S. military began its occupation of Japan, *The Mikado* was performed for the first time in Japan at the Ernie Pyle Theatre. It should be obvious what the intent of the Occupation authorities was in having this operetta put on. Under the policy of "transforming" the Emperor into a human being, it was highly useful to publicize the operetta's image of the "Mikado" as comical, familiar, and thus very human—not at all divine.

The costumes that were used in this production were truly wonderful, and according to a friend, one set of costumes was actually borrowed from the Imperial household. Even though the performance was put on by order of the American military, I think that in it we can see evidence of a mutual understanding and agreement between the Imperial family and the Occupation authorities, established through the proclamation of January 1946 and the subsequent Imperial tour of the nation, in the effort to show that the Emperor was merely human. Nevertheless, since it was necessary for Japanese to have special permission to attend the performance at the Ernie Pyle Theatre, there cannot have been very many Japanese who actually saw the operetta at that time.

The first time the Japanese really came in contact with *The Mikado* was in June of 1947. It is said that the first Japanese performance was at the Tokyo Theatre by the Nagato Miho opera troupe, under the overall direction of Mr. Itō Michirō. Around that time, a lot of bars and taverns with names that were taken from the operetta opened up, which indicates that the operetta was quite popular at first. However, I have never heard that it was a big hit and had a long run of performances, so it seems that it was a temporary fad. And since the end of the Occupation in 1952, *The Mikado* has not been performed again in Japan.

19

Observing the Tokyo War Crimes Trials

Here I would like to talk about my experience of attending the Tokyo International Military Tribunal for the Far East—what the Japanese call the "Tokyo Trials"—as an observer.

I think it was in July of 1946 that I conceived the desire to attend the Tribunal, after I read in the newspaper that the Soviets were going to call Pu Yi, the "puppet emperor" of Manchukuo, as a witness at the tribunal. Actually, when the Tokyo Trials began in May 1946, an international prosecutorial agency headed by the American Joseph Keenan had requested the Soviet Union to present Pu Yi to give testimony at the tribunal. However, at first the Soviet Union gave no response to this request from Keenan, and they seemed to have no intention of complying. Chief Prosecutor Keenan repeated the request many times, "I want to summon Pu Yi. He is an important witness."

Keenan wanted to obtain important evidence for the prosecution regarding what went on behind the scenes in the establishment of Manchukuo, by the Japanese military, in order to prove that Japan was carrying out a plot to seize China. As the emperor of Manchukuo, Pu Yi could be expected to be very familiar with the inside history of this "nation-building" enterprise.

Pu Yi himself was captured in Manchuria at the same time as the Soviet Union entered the war, in August 1945, and he was taken to the Soviet Union as a war criminal. That is also the reason Keenan requested that the USSR bring him to Tokyo for questioning at the war crimes tribunal.

When I saw Pu Yi's name in the newspaper, it brought back memories of my stamp-collecting days in my youth, when I collected stamps connected with Manchukuo with particular enthusiasm. Come to think of it, one of the things that first attracted me to Asia was the Manchurian Incident and stamps from "Manchukuo."

One day in the first ten days of August 1946, a Soviet aircraft flew into Tokyo from Vladivostok and landed at the Atsugi Airfield, and who should step out of the plane but Pu Yi.

Of course, that is not to say that anyone knew the precise arrival time of the plane or where it would land. It is just that I saw a picture of Pu Yi getting out of the plane, escorted in front and behind by four Soviet soldiers carrying weapons under their arms, and read a newspaper article about the matter. Pu Yi was immediately taken by car to GHQ, where a Soviet delegation was waiting.

Incidentally, at the end of December 1945 I left the department for translating letters to MacArthur, and at the time of Pu Yi's arrival I was responsible for the daily reproduction of the English translations of the Japanese press.

On the day after arriving in Tokyo, the Soviet side, it was said, conveyed to Chief Prosecutor Keenan that they wanted to put Pu Yi on the witness stand immediately. The reason given was that "Pu Yi can stay in Tokyo only for a week, and after that he must be taken back to the Soviet Union." According to the original schedule of the tribunal, in July 1946 absolutely no investigation had been carried out regarding Pu Yi, so this sudden proposal by the Soviets required a drastic change in the schedule. So Prosecutor Joseph Keenan made a strong appeal to the Australian, Sir William Webb, chief judge of the Military Tribunal for the Far East, that Pu Yi be questioned as a witness as soon as possible. Webb accepted the appeal and decided on August 16 as the day for Pu Yi's questioning.

When I read this newspaper report, I was extremely excited. Ever since I had seen Pu Yi's name, I had become extremely interested in the War Crimes Tribunal, and when I read that he was going to appear as a witness, this interest reached a peak. I resolved that no matter what, I must go and hear his testimony.

Needless to say, I made every effort possible to obtain an observer's pass. I managed to obtain a pass from August 1st, and when the 16th came, I saw Pu Yi for the first time with my own eyes. The place that was being used for the War Crimes Tribunal courtroom was originally the building that housed the former Ministry of the Army, though of course the interior of the building had been redecorated to look like a courtroom.

The courtroom was a large rectangular room, on one side of which, on high seats, sat the judges appointed by each Allied country, presided over by Sir William Webb. The accused occupied seats in a large box on the other side facing the judges. There were numbers on the box identifying each accused war criminal.

On the observer's pass that I obtained, the names of the judges were listed on the left, and the numbers and names of the defendants were listed on the right, so that it resembled a card for a baseball match between the Yankees and the Braves or the Royals and the Indians. I looked at the card and identified each one of the defendants. "Oh, here is Hiranuma, and there is Shimada. . . ."

However, even though the defendants sat at the same set place day after day, there were some absentees, like Ōkawa Shūmei, who was suffering from cerebral syphilis and at one point had hit Tōjō Hideki in the head and was ordered to leave the courtroom. Thus, one will notice on the photograph of my pass that Ōkawa's name does not appear. We observers sat in a balcony overlooking the courtroom, and we listened intently during the course of the trial, while looking out over the judges on our left and the defendants on our right. To pursue the baseball analogy, it was just like watching the game from the stands.

Between the judges' seats and the defendants' seats, there were the seats of the lawyers for both sides, and right in the middle there was a table with microphones, at which a large team of simultaneous translators was at work.

The languages used in the tribunal were English, French, Russian, and Japanese. The Soviet judge spoke only Russian. The French judge spoke only French. On the other hand, the Chinese and Dutch judges also understood English, as did the judges from the Philippines and India. Thus, adding the Japanese spoken by the defendants, there were a total of four languages flying around the courtroom. The translation from and into all these languages, needless to say, required the work of a great number of simultaneous interpreters.

To translate the verbal exchanges going on in the courtroom was an extremely difficult job, and because there was also special content where special vocabulary was required, almost all of the interpreters sent by the American army were Japanese-American non-commissioned or commissioned officers.

The progress of the trial was horribly slow. Because their work was extremely exhausting, the interpreters on duty were changed every thirty minutes. The interpretation was sometimes simultaneous, and sometimes, for reasons I did not really understand, consecutive.

The day that I went as an observer was precisely the day that Pu Yi gave his testimony. When I arrived at the observers' seats, he was already on the witness stand being cross-examined by a lawyer. The lawyer handling the cross-examination was Kiyose Ichirō, who became internationally famous as the lawyer for Tōjō Hideki and went on to become Speaker of the Diet.

Kiyose asked Pu Yi, "I think you know the Confucian classics. According to the Book of . . . the government is. . ."

Since Pu Yi was a Chinese member of the former Imperial family who had received a Confucian education since his childhood, he must have known the passage that Kiyose quoted from the classics. While this exchange was going on, suddenly the chief judge, Webb, hit his gavel on the desk and cut short Kiyose's cross-examination. "What on earth is this cross-examination? Why are you asking such questions? What does this tribunal have to do with the Confucian classics? Move forward with the cross-examination!"

Listening to this dialogue between Kiyose and Pu Yi through his earphones, Webb apparently got extremely angry. Not only Kiyose, but Pu Yi himself seemed very surprised at this sudden burst of anger. For the rest of the afternoon, rather than a cross-examination of Pu Yi, the proceedings were more like an argument between Kiyose and Webb over the nature of the cross-examination. Yet I understood well why it was that Kiyose had brought up the Confucian classics and began by going after Pu Yi from this angle. Kiyose's plan of attack was to demonstrate that Pu Yi knew the Confucian classics very well, and then demonstrate that the government of "Manchukuo" could be legitimized on the basis of the Confucian classics. If so, that would prove that the state of "Manchukuo" was not just a conspiracy on the part of Japan, and that Pu Yi was not just a "puppet emperor." So that is why he brought up the Confucian classics. Pu Yi could hardly say that he did not know the Confucian classics.

Yet Sir William Webb had absolutely no conception of the meaning of the Confucian classics in East Asian political culture, so he was completely unable to comprehend Kiyose's intention. Not only could he not comprehend it, but he obviously thought it was a silly waste of time. Accordingly, regardless of Kiyose's objections, he asked repeatedly, "What connection do the Confucian classics have with this tribunal?" and he ordered Kiyose to make it short. Finally, he said to Kiyose, "Return to your seat! I don't think there is any need to discuss this matter any more."

Now I am certainly not trying to characterize the whole picture of the Tokyo War Crimes Tribunal on the basis of one exchange I happened to hear as an observer on this one day. But this sort of exchange does seem to have occurred quite frequently in the parts of the tribunal that I observed. The "Tokyo Trials" themselves went on for a very long time, and the process of judgment itself was extremely intricate, reflecting the complex nature of the international situation at the time. So the judgment of Pu Yi was only one small piece of the whole picture.

Nevertheless, whether we call it a difference of cultures or a language barrier, it did seem that the two sides were sorely lacking in the capacity to understand each other. For example, the Australian, Sir William Webb, may have been well versed in Anglo-Saxon culture, but he had no education in East Asian culture that would have made it possible for him to understand Kiyose's line of reasoning, and what is more, all conversation by both sides was done only through interpreters, so it was not the sort of situation where one party could have a heart-to-heart with the other party. The fact that Webb was ill-disposed toward Kiyose, I think, only resulted in a further intensification of this cultural and linguistic barrier.

Truly, watching the exchange between the two sides from the observers' seats, the progress was so slow as to put one into a daze. Webb would say something in English. Kiyose would put his earphones to his ears and listen to the Japanese translation of Webb's words. Nodding his head, when he had finished listening to the translation, Kiyose would take off his earphones and reply to Webb's words in Japanese. Webb would put the earphones to his ears and listen to the English translation of what Kiyose had said. As this went on, due probably to the mode of translation and the cultural gap, the conversation would often go back and forth and fail to move forward at all, getting far more complicated and involved than was necessary. While this sort of exchange was going on repeatedly, a week passed by in a flash, and Pu Yi disappeared from the courtroom and was taken back to the Soviet Union.

My involvement with the Tokyo Trials was limited to this one incident with Pu Yi. Finally, though it has nothing to do with the Tokyo Trials, let me relate a bit about my experience of observing the Allied Council for Japan. The Allied Council for Japan was something created as a "Tokyo version" of the Far Eastern Commission in Washington. Originally, the Far Eastern Commission was one of the items agreed upon in 1945 between Soviet Foreign Minister Molotov and American Secretary of State Byrnes. The Soviet Union, in exchange for their approval of MacArthur's assuming the post of Supreme

Commander for the Allied Powers, agreed to the establishment of a Far Eastern Commission in Washington. The idea was that, by installing Soviet representatives there, they could observe, censure, and object to the actions of MacArthur in Tokyo.

But because it was established in Washington, far removed from Tokyo, it is hardly necessary to say that the effectiveness of its "observation" was not very high. That is precisely why the U.S. had the committee set up in Washington. For this reason, the problem for the U.S. was the "Tokyo version," or the field outpost, so to speak, of the committee in Washington, namely the four-power Allied Council for Japan. The Soviet Union, as one of the Allies, had sent its representatives to the council, along with representatives of the U.S., China, and the British Commonwealth. China, needless to say, was represented by the KMT. The first meeting of this Allied Council for Japan was held in the Meiji Seimei Building in April, 1946. I think that it was held in the Executive Conference Room or some such room in the building, as I recall that it was a very beautifully decorated room.

General Courtney Whitney, representing General MacArthur, took the chairman's seat as the U.S. representative. Since it was determined that the U.S. would permanently occupy the chairmanship of the council, the U.S. was able to steer the council and make resolutions as it saw fit. When the council would be convened, who would be asked to speak, and who would be prevented from speaking—all of these were determined completely by the American representative. In this way, no doubt, the U.S. hoped, in effect, to maintain sole control of the occupation of Japan.

At any rate, when General Whitney appeared at the first meeting of the council, he read a statement from General MacArthur and formally proclaimed the opening of the conference. Following that, each of the other member countries' representatives read a statement, first China, then the Soviet Union, then the British Commonwealth.

In their opening statements, the representatives of each of these countries presented the areas within the Occupation plan with which they were strongly concerned. The representative of China emphasized the problem of the *zaibatsu* (monopolistic industrial and financial combines); the representative of the Soviet Union emphasized the labor problem; the representative of the British Commonwealth emphasized the problem of agricultural land reform, and so on.

This was all there was, and the meeting of the council was concluded without making any substantial plans. The second meeting was more or less the same as the first. The pattern established at the first meeting became the model for all subsequent meetings. SCAP continued to ignore the opinions regarding the reform program that were submitted at the meetings of the Allied Council for Japan. This attitude pertained to all of the member countries, and not just the Soviet Union. The U.S. continued to ignore the opinions of China (the KMT government) and the British Commonwealth, just as they continued to ignore those of the Soviet Union.

That is to say, SCAP continued to hold onto absolute authority with regard to the policies to be followed in the Occupation of Japan. In that sense, the Allied Council for Japan must have appeared as something antagonistic to that absolute authority. For that reason, it would be better to say that SCAP was determined from the start to ignore the Allied Council for Japan, and thus the Allied Council was unable to perform any substantial function. Even if the discussion at the council meetings became tangled and confused, the U.S. representative continued to grope for a way to ignore the discussion and the suggestions offered therein by the member countries. In the year that I stayed in Japan, I saw with my own eyes that the Allied Council for Japan was an entity that existed in name only, without substance, and that this situation only became more severe as time went on.

Returning to America

EVERYTHING I SAW and heard in Japan while I was there during the Occupation was totally new to me, and it left me with a very strong impression. It was during the summer of 1946 that I decided I wanted to return to the U.S. and resume my studies at university.

It is not that I was starting to dislike Japan. But I had been in the army for four years, and, frankly speaking, I had become a bit fed up with army life. On top of that, I was approaching the age of twenty-two, and I was concerned about whether it was getting too late to return to university.

Unlike today, when most universities have a two-semester system, one from January and one from September, American universities at the time had only one time for admission, early September. Accordingly, if I was going to return to university, I would have to be back at Princeton by early September. As I mentioned at the beginning of this book, I had kept my place at

Princeton when I entered the army Japanese language training program.

No matter what, I thought, I will return to university within the present year. It was June when I made this decision. There was only a little more than two months left before the new academic year would begin in September. I would have to get cracking. I explained the situation to my superior officer, seeking his agreement, and then called my father and told him my plans. In order to assure that my military duties would proceed smoothly, I also wrote a letter to my representative in Congress requesting a discharge. In the two months after I made my decision, I did everything possible to assure that I could return stateside and resume my university studies.

However, my superior officer did not accept my appeal. He ignored my desire to return to the U.S. and told me to stay in Japan. Needless to say, I did not accept his refusal. I voiced my disagreement personally to that superior officer and objected repeatedly. Then I told my colleagues about my dissatisfaction and continued to seek a way to make it possible for me to return to the U.S. My request was finally approved on October 1, 1946, which, of course, was already too late from the point of view of my original plan.

But I did not give up. Still searching for any possibility that might open for me, I left Yokohama Harbor and headed across the ocean. Of course, the sea journey was very slow, and in view of my urgency to get back to the U.S. this made me very impatient. When I finally arrived on the west coast, I immediately boarded a train and headed directly for Chicago.

Here I went through the formal procedures of getting my discharge, putting my documents in order, getting a physical examination, collecting my insurance certificate and my pay. With this and that to take care of, the whole procedure of getting my discharge took about one week. No matter how much I rushed, it just required that much time.

As a result, it was not until the end of October that I finished all the official proceedings and was able to be reunited with my family in Cleveland. I was too late to return to Princeton for the 1946–1947 academic year. So, finding myself suddenly with a lot of time on my hands, I took the opportunity to take a trip to Florida for fun. I wanted to get my feelings in order and work out a new plan of attack. After much consideration, I decided to apply for special permission to return to my studies in the middle of the academic year.

In January, 1947, I obtained special permission to re-enter Princeton. While this meant admission in the middle of the academic year, such a measure had already been adopted in the case of other demobilized students. So I succeeded in getting back into my undergraduate studies. However, frankly speaking, in comparison to my time at the Army Intensive Japanese Language School, the university lectures were not up to the level I had expected, and among my classmates I did not find anyone whom I really thought was especially talented.

I guess this was because I was now older than the majority of the students. Through my training in the army and my wartime experience, not to mention my experience in the Occupation as a lieutenant in charge of a department of ATIS that employed many Japanese people, and so on, it seemed that I had become much more of an adult than the general run of students. At any rate, I could not help seeing the students around me as rather childish.

What is more, because I was concentrating on my studies in order to make up for the portion of the academic year I had lost, in comparison with those students who were enjoying life while being students I was more thirsty and greedy for knowledge.

Because my everyday life was quite tense, I felt that the lectures I had to attend every day were somehow not really satisfying.

In June of 1948 I graduated from Princeton, just somewhat more than a year after I had resumed my studies. To look back on it all, I had entered Princeton as a freshman in the autumn of 1942, and in the spring of 1943 I left the university to join the army. After four years of army life in 1947 I returned to my studies, and then I graduated in June 1948. I was able to graduate after only a bit more than a year because the university gave me credit for the training I had had at the Army Intensive Japanese Language School. Because of that, I had no need to earn credits in a foreign language, which reduced my burden by about 30 credits. So I was able to graduate in an unusually short time.

At the same time as I graduated from Princeton in June, 1948, I entered the graduate school of the University of Michigan. Since both the graduation and the admission were in the same month, it was quite literally "at the same time." In June of 1949, I obtained my Master of Arts degree in Far Eastern Studies. The reader may think that this should read 1950, but it is true that I actually completed my M.A. in only a year. Of course, in those days, like now, it normally took two years or more to complete a master's course. However, I used the summer vacation period to the full to earn credits, so I was able to accumulate all the credits I needed in one year. At the same time as I completed my M.A., I commenced my Ph.D. program. And finally, I obtained my doctorate in history in 1955. Since it took me almost six years to complete a Ph.D. program, compared with the fast pace at which I finished up my B.A. and M.A. courses, it might seem that I really took my time with my Ph.D.

Actually, I myself think that I took it pretty slow. However, during this time I spent one year studying in Holland on a

Fulbright scholarship, so the Ph.D. itself was actually completed in a little less than five years. But even then, I cannot deny that I was taking my time.

Of course that does not mean that there was no reason for this. For about a year I was helping my father with his work. During that year, I wanted to consider thoroughly whether I should go on to be a businessman or a university teacher. "There is no need to rush," I thought. "It is a question of my whole life. I will stay here for a while and consider the matter slowly and carefully." For a year I suppressed my desire to rush ahead and did a thorough reexamination of myself.

Finally I discussed the matter with my thesis supervisor, Professor John W. Hall, and his answer was, "Push forward single-mindedly on the path that you yourself wish to follow."

So at last I made up my mind and poured all of my energy into the task of completing my doctoral thesis and obtaining my doctorate. The title of my thesis was *The Dutch Impact on Japan (1640–1853)*. The thesis examined the influence of Holland on Japan up to the time of the opening of the country in the mid-nineteenth century, focusing on the role of Edo-period Dutch learning (Rangaku).

I wrote my thesis while shutting myself up in my parents' home in Cleveland. I think it took me about a year to write it. There is no particular reason why I wrote it at my parents' house. It was not just that it allowed me to save on rent and living expenses, but also that there was a study in the house and it was a comfortable environment. I mailed my completed thesis to my supervisor a chapter at a time, and after each submission I received comments from him by letter. So the only time I showed my face at the university in Ann Arbor was when I went for my oral defense, the last stage in the process of obtaining my degree.

I was awarded the Ph.D. degree at the university in June 1955. In 1986 I published a book called *Japan: The Dutch Experience* (The Athlone Press), which was based on my thesis plus research done on the topic subsequently, so it represents, so to speak, a significant part of my life's work.

I returned from Japan and resumed my studies in 1947. I obtained my doctorate in 1955. That means a total of eight years that I spent finishing my pre-doctorate degrees, fulfilling the doctoral course requirements, and writing my thesis. As I mentioned above, my impression on returning to university, to put it simply, was that I had become very much an adult, and the students around me all seemed rather childish, far less interesting and talented than the friends I had in my days at the Army Intensive Japanese Language School. Generally speaking, the students who were demobilized after serving in the war and returned to school were of a higher caliber, more motivated and serious, and they had clear objectives and a clear idea of what profession they wanted to devote their lives to.

One could say that the cream of the crop of the American youth of that period were those who went off to the war and fought for their country and for the cause of democracy. And those from among this "cream of the crop" who were lucky enough to survive the war, when they returned exchanged their guns for pens and devoted themselves to study. It is not surprising that they were excellent students.

Accordingly, among the comrades who worked together with me in the military, especially among those who were my classmates at the Army Intensive Japanese Language School and returned to do research at the University of Michigan after the war, there were many highly talented men, many of whom played an important role in American society and academia for many years thereafter.

There was Edward Norbeck at Rice University, John Cornell at the University of Texas, George Shea at the University of Minnesota, Robert Brower, head of the Department of East Asian Languages at the University of Michigan, George Totten of the University of Southern California, and many others.

I would also like particularly to single out Professor Joseph K. Yamagiwa of the University of Michigan for the quality of his character and cultural education, the depth of his mastery of Japanese, and his incomparable skill in Japanese language education. Under his direction, a large number of Japan scholars were born, and those who had studied under him were active on the front lines of Japan Studies in America for many decades.

*　*　*

My second visit to Japan was in 1958, that is, twelve years after I had left to return to Princeton. My third trip to Japan was in 1964, the year of the Tokyo Olympics. Since then, with the exception of 1975–76, I visited Japan every year, and while working on my research, I witnessed with astonishment the intensity of changes that Japan was going through.

Yet, even though I was there almost every year, I found the changes so rapid and drastic that they are difficult to describe. The year from 1945 to 1946, when I first set foot on the land of Japan and worked as a second lieutenant and then a first lieutenant in the army was a short period, and I had no basis of comparison. Everything was a burned-out wasteland, the postwar recovery was just beginning, and those buildings that did survive the bombing were all remnants of prewar Japan.

During my second visit in 1958, the postwar recovery had progressed to a very noticeable extent, and I was able to see a new and very different postwar Japan taking shape before my eyes.

On my third visit in 1964, the vestiges of wartime Japan had disappeared completely, and only the shape of the new postwar Japan presented itself before my eyes. Superhighways and sky-scrapers. Forests of buildings sprouting up all over the place. I was astounded at the rapidity of the change. I think that in comparison with the intensity of the changes that I witnessed on my third visit, the changes I had seen in my second visit were nothing.

A New Japan, where everything has changed so drastically. "America's Japan," whose first year was 1945–1946, has continued to go through intense changes right up to the present day, and one can say with certainty that it will continue to change in fundamental ways in the twenty-first century. But what a privilege it was to be there and see with my own eyes the very first birth of this new Japan, when the great forces that would eventually bring about these vast changes were just beginning to take form!

INDEX

✪

Note: Page numbers in *italics* indicate photos in the insert section. As in the text, Japanese names are rendered as family name followed by given name, with no comma.

★ ★ ★

Agricultural land reform, 67–68
Allied Council for Japan, 136–39
Allied Translator and
    Interpreter Section: hiring
    Japanese translators, 44–47;
    in Philippines, 26, 33–35;
    suicides within, 106–11; in
    Tokyo, 37–43, 44–47
Alweis, Lt. Frank, 59
Ammunition, hidden, 54
Army Intensive Japanese
    Language School, 2, 3, *4*,
    9–21, 145

Atomic bombs, 31, 108

Bataan, 62
Beheading of American
    prisoners, 94–95
Bolshevik Revolution, refugees
    from, 114
Brower, Robert, 146
Burma, Prime Minister of (Ba
    Maw), 54, 58–60
Byrnes, James, 136

Camp Perry, Ohio, 9–10

Cannibalism of American prisoners, 92–94
Cathay Mansions Hotel, Shanghai, 113
China, in Allied Council for Japan, 137–38
Christianity: "boom" in, 104–5; MacArthur's promotion of, 66–67
Civil Information and Education Section, romanized Japanese characters and, 82
Communist influence in Shanghai, 117–18
Constitution, 69–79; vs. American constitution, 76–79; American views of, 70–71; chronologic development of, 71–76; current form of, 79; MacArthur's ideas on, 65–66; promulgation of, 75
Constitutions of the World, 74
Cornell, John, 146
Corregidor, 62

Daiichi Hotel, 37–38
Daiichi Seimei Building, MacArthur's headquarters in, 38, 41–42, 53, 64–65
Democracy: MacArthur mission for, 65–66; study of, 97–99, 102–3; Taisho period, 71
Demonstrations, 80–82
Densha (street car), 100–101
Dictionaries, 14, 30

Diet opening, Emperor attending, 122

Education: English language schools for, 97–103; romanized Japanese characters in, 82
Election provisions, in constitution, 77
Emperor Kumazawa, 85–90
Emperor system: defects of, 102–3; humanity vs. god-like stature, 122–24; *The Mikado* and, 122–29; necessity of, 123; as symbol, 73, 76
English language: in children's books, 84; conversation schools for, 97–103; Japanese people speaking, 39–40
Entertainment: *The Mikado*, 122–29; movies, 16, 29, 116
Ernie Pyle Theater, Tokyo, 6, 124, 128–29

Far Eastern Commission, 137
Feudalism, abolition of, 73
Food shortage, 48–50
Fort McClellan, Alabama, 5, 18
Fort Snelling, Minnesota, 19–22
Freedoms: in constitution, 77; demonstrations resulting from, 80–82
Fujiya Hotel, Miyanoshita, 48
Fulbright scholarship, 144
Fushimi-no-miya, 128

General strike of February 1, 1947, 81
Gifts: from Goodman's students, 99–100; for MacArthur and family, 55–57
Gilbert, W. S., lyricist of *The Mikado*, 122–29
Goodman, Grant, *1, 4, 5*; at Army Intensive Japanese Language School, 2, 3, *4*, 9–21, 145; arrival in Japan, 36–37; on constitution, 69–79; early interest in Asia, 1–3; Fulbright scholarship of, 144; on General MacArthur, 61–68; graduate studies of, 143–45; in Philippines, 23–30, 33–35; practical army training of, 18–22; Princeton University studies of, 4–8, 140–43; return to America, 140–42; return visits to Japan, 146–47; Shanghai vacation of, 112–18; stamp collection of, 3; at Tokyo Trials, 130–39; at Yokohama Court, 91–96
Gordon, Beate Sirota, 73
Gorer, Geoffrey, 14

Hall, John W., 144
Hall, Robert B., 11
Hara-kiri, 94, 95
Hata Ikuhiko, MacArthur book by, 61
Higashikuni cabinet, 72

Hirohito, Emperor, 122–24
Hiroshima atomic bomb, 31, 108
Hitti, Philip, 6–7
Hot springs, 48–49
Human rights (in Japanese constitution), 75–77

Imai Toshiki, 99
Infantry training, 18
Inflation, in shanghai, 114–16
Innes, Arthur Rose, 14
International Christian University, 66
Internment camps, 12
Invitations, to MacArthur, 55
Itō Michirō, 129

James, Clayton, MacArthur book by, 61
Japan: The Dutch Experience, 145
Japan-America Conversation Academy, 97–103
Japanese language: Australian schools for, 26; British schools for, 26; in broadcasts, 19; dead words in, 100; dictionaries for, 14, 30; military vocabulary for, 19; in movies, 16, 29; romanization of, 82–84; scripts for, 19; in songs, 16

Kades, Col. Charles, 73, 74, 78
Kanji, replacement with romanized characters, 80–82